The KINGDOM of HEAVEN is at Hand

RICK JOYNER

with small group discussion questions

The Kingdom of Heaven is at Hand
by Rick Joyner
Copyright © 2023

Distributed by MorningStar Publications, Inc.,
A division of MorningStar Fellowship Church
375 Star Light Drive, Fort Mill, SC 29715
www.MorningStarMinistries.org
1-800-542-0278

Unless otherwise indicated, all Scripture quotations are taken from the New American Standard Version, copyright © 1995 by Thomas Nelson, Inc.

No part of this book may be reproduced or transmitted in any form or by any means electronic or mechanical, including photocopying, recording, or by any information storage and retrieval system, without written permission from the author(s).

All rights reserved.

Printed in the United States of America
Cover and layout design by Michael Fickess

ISBN—978-1-60708-003-9

For a free catalog of MorningStar Resources,
please call 1-800-542-0278

TABLE OF CONTENTS

ONE | SEEKING FIRST HIS KINGDOM
- 5 -

TWO | TOUCHING HIS KINGDOM IN NEW WAYS
- 15 -

THREE | PLANTING THE SEEDS OF HIS KINGDOM
- 23 -

FOUR | MAKING "SHEEP NATIONS" IN HIS KINGDOM
- 33 -

FIVE | TRAINING TO REIGN IN HIS KINGDOM
- 43 -

SIX | PREPARING THE WAY FOR HIS KINGDOM
- 53 -

SEVEN | LOOKING FOR THE SIGNS OF HIS KINGDOM
- 65 -

EIGHT | APPROACHING THE KING OF KINGS
- 79 -

NINE | PURSUING, KNOWING, AND LOVING THE KING
- 85 -

TEN | LEARNING HOW TO APPROACH THE KING
- 91 -

ELEVEN | DISCERNING OUR ROLE IN HIS KINGDOM
- 99 -

TWELVE | THE WEIGHTIEST MATTER
- 109 -

SEEKING FIRST HIS KINGDOM

1

Jesus repeatedly said, "the kingdom of God is at hand." This statement is as much about location as it is time. His kingdom is so close we can touch it, but more than seeing or touching it, we can enter it and live in it, regardless of what's happening in our world.

In Matthew 11:12, Jesus said, **"From the days of John the Baptist until now the kingdom of heaven suffers violence, and violent men take it by force."** The Greek words translated "violence" and "violent" here are usually translated "pressure" or "force." This implies that the resolute and forceful ones are the ones taking the kingdom. The passive may seem devout but are missing the greatest opportunity of eternity.

The Lord exhorted that those who seek will find, those who ask will receive, and those who knock will have doors opened to them. In the original Greek language, this reads, those who keep seeking, asking, and knocking will receive. Thus, love and faith, the most powerful spiritual forces in the New Testament, are both action words.

In I Corinthians 14:1, we are exhorted to **"desire earnestly spiritual gifts."** Those who are just "open" to receiving them never do. If we do not esteem them according to their infinite value and pursue them as earnestly as they deserve, we should not expect to receive them. What makes a treasure a treasure is that it is either rare or difficult to obtain. Treasures do not grow on trees or simply show up. We must esteem spiritual gifts and pursue them like the great treasures that they are. Still, we are exhorted to seek His kingdom first. This must be our highest priority.

When the Lord said, "the kingdom suffers violence" (or force), He did not mean "suffers" in the sense of something bad happening but "suffers" in the sense of allowing something to be done. In other words, God allows the forceful to take the kingdom. The question is, do we love His kingdom enough to be this resolute?

Jesus also said this gospel of the kingdom would be preached in all the world before He and His kingdom would come (see Matthew 24:14). What has been preached since the first century has only been a small part of the gospel of the kingdom, the gospel of salvation. The gospel of salvation is without question an important part of the gospel of the kingdom and it is so awesome that some are happy to camp there, but it's only one part of the gospel we must preach in all the world. The gospel of salvation is man-centered; the gospel of the kingdom is God-centered. It's all about the King and His domain coming to earth.

In Luke 17:20-21 Jesus said, **"The kingdom of God is not coming with signs to be observed; nor will they say, 'Look, here it is!' or, 'There it is!' For behold, the kingdom of God is in your midst."** Many have been expecting and looking for another great awakening. However, it is becoming clear that another great awakening has already been going on for some time now, yet few have recognized it. Few can see His kingdom even when it is close to them. We must understand how something so deep and so wide could be happening in our midst, yet so few see it, including those who have been expecting and looking for it.

Another reason we must understand this is because this has become a pattern throughout church history. Those who have been a part of a move of God have almost always ended up not recognizing but also persecuting the next move of God. If we understood the causes of this, perhaps we could avoid it. How much more could be accomplished if there was a movement that did not have to stop moving or become distracted by those who are resisting it?

A remarkable move of God is happening right now in America and other nations unlike any move of God we have experienced or even contemplated. It is deep below the surface and does not seem to be led by any group, ministry, church, or personality. Multitudes are turning to biblical morality and values without even knowing what they are. It's like the **"law written in their hearts" (see Romans 2:15)** that God put in all men is being awakened on a huge scale in people who do not yet know the Lord as their Redeemer and Savior.

If we considered the media a reflection of what is really happening, we would think the opposite is happening. Thankfully, most people now realize what is presented in the media is often the opposite of, or at least a variant of, the truth. Just as our media is increasingly out of touch with reality, our political leaders are increasingly out of touch with the people they are supposed to represent. Morally speaking, most Americans are now moving in the opposite direction from where their leaders are trying to take them.

The same could be said of our spiritual leaders and perhaps leaders in every field. What is happening can only be explained as something sovereign. I am not aware of anyone who has tried to create what we are now seeing unfold.

Jamie Buckingham once told a group of writers who had gathered, "Our job is to find out which way the Holy Spirit is moving and get there first to set up a book table!" We all laughed, but it was the truth. We need to discern how and where the Holy Spirit is moving and prepare the spiritual food that people will need. We need to prepare in other ways as well.

We should not be too disappointed, however. Has there ever been an example in Scripture or in history when God moved in a sovereign way and people were ready for it? Even in the parable of the ten virgins, the so-called "wise virgins" were sleeping when the Bridegroom came. However, they had oil in their lamps, so they were more prepared than the "foolish virgins." This new awakening is a very deep, wide, and powerful movement that almost no one saw coming and few yet see. However, they will see.

One way this movement is beginning to manifest itself is in patriotic movements in various countries that are seeking to restore their culture and heritage which has been assaulted by globalists. I was told by the Lord back in 2014, "Patriotism is going to win," and not just in the U.S.

Larry Randolph once said, "One of the names of God should be 'Jehovah Sneaky.'" The Holy Spirit loves to sneak up on us and seems committed to doing things in ways we do not expect. Not that He is trying to trick us so much as this is His nature. He is the Creator who made everyone, every leaf, and every snowflake different. Likewise, in the Gospels, it seems He never healed or did anything the same way twice.

Since creativity is God's nature, becoming an "old wineskin" that is too rigid or inflexible to receive His new wine is one major reason we who were once used by Him begin to oppose the next move of God. And one reason we become old wineskins is we build our expectations of the future on the past rather than on the unyielding pursuit of Him.

However, since history testifies that God never moved the same way twice, we are much more likely to miss what He is doing today. Instead, we should honor and study how He has moved in the past, so we can learn and prepare for what He is doing and will do. Such accounts help build our faith and teach us His ways, but they won't help us much if we abuse this knowledge by expecting Him to do things the same way the next time. In fact, doing so, will keep us far removed the next time He moves.

The unique ways God loves to move should not disturb us. If anything, it should keep our relationship with Him fresh and exciting. God never changes, but to us He is "new every morning" because He is so unique, diverse, and creative we are constantly seeing "new" aspects of Him that are only new to us. This is what makes walking with God the greatest adventure one can live, and for those who love adventure, this is great. However, to the timid and rigid, this is frightening. This brings us to this challenge every believer must face—will we live by faith in Him or by fear?

I started studying church history, revivals, and moves of God more than fifty years ago. One common characteristic I have found in every move is that they are all unique. There is still much we can gain from studying the past, but not if we seek a formula or pattern for how He will move the next time.

Keep in mind, using formulas and patterns to see into the future is a form of witchcraft. Instead, the true Christian life is to live with the most unique and creative One there ever has been, is, or ever will be. Thus, a love for God's creativity and diversity is required.

The First Great Awakening was unique in history. There has never been a move of God like it before or since. The Second Great Awakening could not have been more different from the first. And what is now unfolding is profoundly different from either, yet it is the beginning of a similar nationwide and worldwide awakening.

As we study the evidence that this is happening, and how it is happening, we will need wisdom from above on how to respond to it. How can we have the resolute forcefulness required to take the kingdom without the presumptions that would bring confusion or distraction to what the Holy Spirit is doing?

One thing we can be sure of is we will not do this perfectly. Perfectionism is one of the worst enemies of spiritual advancement. We are not used by God because we are smart enough, knowledgeable enough, wise enough, or even holy enough. We are only useful to Him to the degree that we trust in Him, in what He has already accomplished, and in His power and authority. Our job is to follow Him closely and to always make ourselves available to Him.

In a recent face-to-face encounter with the Lord, I asked Him, "What is the main thing we can do to help prepare for Your coming kingdom?" He said, "Make disciples." When I asked Him, "How?" He said, "Start." I immediately thought of the law of inertia and how we cannot steer something until it is moving. If we get engaged and start moving, He will steer us!

Let us make seeking first His kingdom our number one resolve. Every time we are distracted from this, we must immediately repent and get back on course. Doing so comes with one of His greatest promises: He will take care of the things that concern us (see Matthew 6:33). He does this much better than we ever could. So, let's resolve this year and every year to obey His command to seek His kingdom first.

CHAPTER ONE
GROUP DISCUSSION QUESTIONS

1. Rick recommends an active pursuit of the Lord and His gifts rather than a passive "openness." What can we do each day to draw closer to the Lord and grow in our spiritual gifts?

2. Rick points out that the Lord often reveals Himself to us in new ways, especially through fresh moves of God that may look different than what has happened in previous revivals. What mindsets do we need to develop to recognize and embrace the new things God will do in our generation?

3. How can we avoid the pitfalls of legalism and perfectionism as we pursue the kingdom of heaven together?

Touching His Kingdom in New Ways

When Jesus walked the earth, He said, **"The kingdom of heaven is at hand" (see Matthew 3:2, 4:17),** meaning it was so close we could touch it. That is our goal—to touch His kingdom in a new way, to bring it into our lives in a new way, and then through our lives, help others touch it.

Every time the Holy Spirit moves or touches a person, they encounter the kingdom of God. A basic devotion of every Christian should be to seek first His kingdom as He commanded, dwell in His kingdom and domain, and proclaim His authority over all things, which is the gospel of the kingdom.

One basic way we enter and abide in His kingdom is through prayer. This is direct communication with God. Since Jesus is the King of kings, the High Priest, and "the only mediator between God and men" (see I Timothy 2:5), we can be sure the Lord's Prayer is also the most effective prayer. When the disciples asked Jesus to teach them to pray, He gave them (and us) the shortest, simplest, most powerful prayer they could pray. One of the most powerful ways the Lord's Prayer can impact *our* daily lives is by beginning each day recounting it.

For some two thousand years, the Lord's Prayer has been prayed by His followers, making it the most repeated prayer of all time. Each time we repeat it, we align ourselves with God's most basic purposes contained within this prayer. Every word powerfully connects us to God's heart for us and for this world. Just the first two words of this prayer are worthy of volumes of commentary—**"Our Father" (see Matthew 6:9).** This raises the level of our appeal beyond that of servants or officials to that of His own sons and daughters!

We could spend a lifetime considering the wonderful nature of these first two words and the unfathomable treasures that come with such access to God, but we must move on to the next phrase, which establishes the most important reason for the prayer—**"Hallowed be Your name" (see Matthew 6:9).** To "hallow" means to sanctify. Since His name *is* holy, we want to treat it with the highest dignity and respect it deserves.

Treating the holy things of God casually brought severe consequences to even the greatest prophet of the Old Testament—Moses. Even in the New Testament, in the book of Acts, we see the fate of Ananias and Sapphira. Our holy God is not to be trifled with. However, we should also not approach God only in fear but with much love and respect as we delight in Him and give Him due honor. He *is* the King and higher than *any* king!

One primary way we can honor the Lord when we draw near to Him is to never presume we can come to Him except by the blood of Jesus. And one way we can honor the sacrifice He made is to come boldly to Him, believing in the power of His blood to thoroughly cleanse our sin and make us fully acceptable to our Father.

We do not have this access privilege because we earned it by our obedience, faithfulness, wisdom, or any exploits He enabled us to perform in His name. We come because we are family, and we treat His name as holy because it is our family name, shared with us by the One who earned it. The only thing we have done or could do is believe in Him and in the power of His name.

Then we come to the main purpose of this greatest of prayers—**"Your kingdom come. Your will be done, on earth as it is in heaven" (Matthew 6:10).** To be aligned with this ultimate purpose of God is key to our own spiritual maturity and usefulness to Him, which is why He commanded us to seek first His kingdom.

One way we can make disciples of nations, as the Great Commission commands, is to lead people to Jesus so they can be born again by His Spirit. As Jesus said, no one can see His kingdom without being born again (see John 3:3). That is why evangelism is a primary devotion of the body of Christ. However, seeing His kingdom is not the same as entering it. By seeking His kingdom first, we can remain on the path of life, grow up into Him, who is King, and thereby be trusted with more of His authority. By walking in His kingdom and lifting up the King, others will be drawn to Him.

Being born into this world is wonderful but only a first step on the path of life. Likewise, being born again is only a first step on our journey with Christ. Just as infants are helpless until they mature, so are we in Christ. We must be born again to see the kingdom of God, yet it is not automatic. Not everyone who is born again sees the kingdom. Just as we must help infants in their first steps of life and development, we must help newborn believers in their first steps of life in Christ, including looking for and seeing His kingdom.

We are born again when we "see" the sacrifice Jesus made for our salvation and trust in Him for our redemption. This is so incomprehensibly wonderful it is easy to see why so many never move beyond this.

However, we must go on to maturity or we will remain helpless spiritual infants instead of workers, builders, messengers, and soldiers of His kingdom. This is how we prepare the way for the coming of the Lord and for His kingdom. Again, the Great Commission is to "make disciples," not just converts.

Basic to being a disciple is doing all things for the Lord. This means we turn everything we do into worship, as we are instructed in Colossians 3:23-24: **"Whatever you do, do your work heartily, as for the Lord rather than for men, knowing that from the Lord you will receive the reward of the inheritance. It is the Lord Christ whom you serve."**

We are not to do our jobs as though we are merely serving men, corporations, organizations, or even great causes, but as though we are serving the King of kings. If every Christian worked with this kind of devotion to excellence in all we do, as the King deserves, we would excel far beyond what we could do otherwise. Everyone would want to hire Christians first, knowing we do our absolute best. However, presently this is not the case, since few Christians live this way, and since few Christians are true disciples.

THE KINGDOM OF HEAVEN IS AT HAND

As Peter Lord said, "The main thing is to keep the main thing the main thing," and serving the King and His kingdom is the main thing for us. We should view everything from a kingdom perspective and keep its interests above all others. We should wake up every day resolving to seek the King above all others. We do this by doing all as worship to Him.

One way we can make great progress in our relationship with the Lord and in His kingdom is by doing what we dislike the most as worship to Him. When we turn drudgery into worship, the drudgery will not remain.

Brother Lawrence is renowned as one of the great souls in history because he once turned the drudgery of dishwashing into worship. This enabled him to abide in the Lord's presence, and in His **"presence is fullness of joy" (see Psalm 16:11).** People from all walks of life came to meet this dishwasher whose life had been so greatly touched by the Lord's presence. He is still, and perhaps forever will be, the most famous dishwasher ever. He washed those dishes with all his heart as unto the Lord.

If we will likewise do the things we are called to do as unto the Lord, we also will come to experience His presence and fullness of joy in them. If we do this, even with the most menial and disliked tasks, we will be transformed ever more when the joy of the Lord and the Lord's presence saturate even the lowest places of our lives, as some of our greatest distractions are eliminated.

Most of us still have a few hundred things wrong with us, and the enemy's strategy is to "wear out the saints" by having us try to focus on fixing them all at once. Breakthroughs happen when we focus on one thing until we overcome it. Doing so can create many other breakthroughs in our lives without even having to focus on them.

Let's focus on one job or one responsibility we do not like, then resolve to do it as unto the Lord. As we see great victories by touching the Lord and His kingdom through these tasks, we will want to conquer other tasks. Even drudgery seems glorious when the joy of the Lord's presence makes drudgery exciting, fulfilling, and a privilege. Then, we will have our own "great awakening." If we do, our lights will burn brightly, and as Leonard Ravenhill often said, "You don't have to advertise a fire!"

CHAPTER TWO
GROUP DISCUSSION QUESTIONS

1. What aspect of Rick's teaching on the Lord's Prayer was most meaningful to you?

2. Rick recommends "doing what we dislike the most" as an act of worship to the Lord. Are there any areas in your life where you feel drudgery, boredom, or dread? How can you invite the Lord into these areas of your life so His light and joy floods in?

3. Rick points out that "every time the Holy Spirit touches a person, they encounter the kingdom of God." Ask the Holy Spirit to highlight one person in your life He wants to touch. Then, take time to intercede for that person and look for an opportunity to minister to them.

PLANTING THE SEEDS OF THE KINGDOM 3

We have addressed how Jesus said the kingdom of heaven is "at hand," meaning it is so close we can touch it. We all must learn to walk in the understanding that if God's kingdom is so close we can touch it, then we must seek to touch it and abide in it every day. From this, we can accomplish our life's mission to go and preach the message of the kingdom and touch everyone we can with it, so they too can become citizens of it.

Next to loving God, we are instructed our main pursuit should be to "seek first the kingdom." If we do this, we are promised everything else will be "added" to us. This is the path toward living the most meaningful, powerful, and exciting life we can live on earth. This is the purpose to which we were called. We are citizens, soldiers, messengers, and ambassadors of another kingdom. Our most important purpose is to be these things, as instructed.

In Daniel 2, the statue that represented man's empires began to crumble when the little stone struck its feet. Then, the little stone grew into a mountain and continued to grow until it filled the whole earth. This falling apart of man's empires is happening now. However, the most important event taking place is the kingdom growing both here and now. We are here to help prepare the way for the Lord by building a highway for His kingdom (see Isaiah 40:3-5).

In Joel 3:14 the prophet declares, **"Multitudes, multitudes in the valley of decision! For the day of the Lord is near in the valley of decision."** He said this **"valley of decision"** is where the day of the Lord is near. This **"valley of decision"** is starting to manifest in various places right now, and we must recognize it when it does. We can see this in the way people are stirred about the issues of the day and troubled that things are not right because their lives are crumbling along with the kingdoms of men upon which they have built their lives. We are here to help them rebuild their lives on a kingdom that *cannot* be shaken. Multitudes are now in this place, ready to come to the Lord.

Ultimately, everyone will pass through this valley of decision and must choose the kingdom in which they will reside. Though the kingdom of God may seem like it is still in the "little stone" phase, it is growing and will not stop growing until it fills the whole earth. One question many ask when they see this is, "Should we continue to be part of the empires of men?" The answer is, "Yes," to the degree that we must call others to turn to the King as well.

In Revelation 11:15, we are told, **"The kingdom of the world has become the kingdom of our Lord and of His Christ; and He will reign forever and ever."** Since the Greek word translated **"has become"** here indicates a transition, many teachers and theologians have considered that God has been sowing seeds of His kingdom into the governments of this world to prepare them for the coming transition. For example, some consider the remarkable message the apostle Paul had for the Athenians regarding "The Unknown God" was an attempt to draw their attention to something God had planted in their heritage long ago, so that it might later bring life to them (see Acts 17:23).

In my travels to the nations, I have looked for similar seeds the Lord had planted in cultures to which I could draw their attention. In some countries, this has had good results, even making their newspapers as messages to their countries. In some places, this bore immediate fruit. In other places, I could not tell if it bore any fruit. Still, we must trust what the Lord said in Isaiah 55:11:

"So will My word be which goes forth from My mouth; it will not return to Me empty without accomplishing what I desire, and without succeeding in the matter for which I sent it."

Just as the apostle Paul sowed God's word into the Athenians, it may not have sprouted then because it was not time. However, at the right time, and with the proper amount of light, heat, and water for growth, this seed no doubt sprouted and bore fruit. As Paul later wrote in I Corinthians 3:6-9:

"I planted, Apollos watered, but God was causing the growth.

"So then neither the one who plants nor the one who waters is anything, but God who causes the growth.

"Now he who plants and he who waters are one; but each will receive his own reward according to his own labor.

"For we are God's fellow workers; you are God's field, God's building."

How much more effective might our evangelistic crusades be if we understood this division of labor? The one sowing the seed would not be stressed about the lack of immediate results from the word preached, knowing others would come later and reap what they had planted, and God would keep score and reap the harvest.

The Lord used the seed metaphor for His message of the kingdom many times and in many ways. In fact, the seed has so many serious implications, we must understand it if we are to fully understand how His kingdom is coming. His kingdom will emerge on earth from the sprouting of all the seeds His messengers have sown.

Seeds need three things to sprout: heat, light, and water. The same is true for the seeds of His kingdom. Heat speaks of the right environment or circumstances. Light speaks of His revelation, since no one will come to the Lord unless the Father draws them. Water speaks of His Word. There must be enough heat and light for a seed to sprout, so the seed will not be fooled into sprouting prematurely during a winter warming period. All three factors must be present for seeds to sprout. If only two of the three are present, seeds will not sprout.

This is a protective mechanism God placed in seeds so they will not sprout before the conditions are right for growth. Again, the same is true with the seeds of the kingdom. We can feel really anointed sharing the gospel with someone, yet nothing may happen immediately, which is fine. If the anointing was there and the words were from God, they will sprout when the conditions are right for that person to grow and bear fruit.

This is why there was such coordination between the apostolic teams in Acts. The apostle Paul understood that when seeds had sprouted and there was ample light and heat for them to grow, they often needed the water of the Word. So, he sent Apollos, Timothy, or other great teachers God had raised up to continue watering the seeds which were sprouting.

We would likely see more fruit in our missions today if we used the same wisdom. The seeds that are sprouting now can become a foundation for the kingdom that will last forever. However, as we are told in the Word, faith must be cultivated. This means there should be regular watering, weeding, fertilizing, etc. We should treat every gathering of the Lord, from the largest congregation to the smallest home group, this way.

Bob Weiner is one such missionary who has been used in remarkable ways to plant kingdom seeds. Not only has his work in many nations raised many thriving churches around the world, but he has also been used to lay foundations in governments to help prepare them for the kingdom. One dramatic place he did this was in Russia.

PLANTING THE SEEDS OF HIS KINGDOM

After the fall of the Iron Curtain, many former Soviet bloc countries were experiencing upheaval during the transition. So, Bob began holding conferences in Moscow, the heart of the former Soviet Union. While preparing one of these conferences, the Lord impressed upon Bob to have his team write a new constitution for Russia, which would help establish their government transition on godly, kingdom principles. Bob took this constitution with him to Moscow and announced at a conference that he would give it to Boris Yeltsin, the new president of Russia. Bob felt led to say this but had no idea how to do it.

After the conference, Bob transferred to another hotel to get rest. While checking in, he noticed preparations were being made for some major event. He was told Boris Yeltsin was coming there that afternoon for a special ceremony. Bob immediately changed into his best clothes, grabbed the constitution he had prepared for Russia, and went to the event. As the receiving lines for Yeltsin were forming, Bob joined one. As he stood there, the Holy Spirit said, "Go to the line on the other side," so he did. Then, Yeltsin walked in with his entourage and walked right up to Bob. Bob grabbed his hand, handed him the constitution, and through interpreters, briefly explained how this could help establish Russia on a path toward freedom and prosperity.

Yeltsin thanked him, told him they were working on a new constitution, and that this could help them. When he left, Yeltsin waved to the people, holding the constitution Bob had just given to him. A short time later, the new constitution of Russia was printed in the newspapers. It contained nearly everything Bob had given him in the constitution.

With the current troubles Russia is facing with its enduring war with Ukraine, one might think Bob's constitution did not accomplish much. However, when the time and the conditions are right, all those seeds God has planted in Russia will begin to sprout. Russia has a major destiny to release one of the greatest moves of God on earth and will become a blazing fire for God. It will be one of the nations that **"become the kingdom of our Lord and His Christ" (see Revelation 11:15)** and will help many other nations to do the same.

The seeds Bob Weiner was able to sow into Russia's future are exceptional. We may see more seeds like this being planted in Russia's future, or we may not. The point is, we often recognize and honor great exploits which deserve to be honored. However, the day-to-day faithfulness of the little seeds no one notices being sown often accomplishes more than all the great exploits combined. We need both.

Many little seeds which have been sown have become determining factors in major decisions and turns of events without even being recognized by those who sowed them. Nevertheless, they will be remembered in the kingdom when the Books of Life are opened. Our goal should be to live faithfully every day, sowing every seed we can—both great and small—while remaining open to being part of the great and remarkable when such opportunities come our way. Regardless, we will find the small things we are faithful to do in the kingdom often have the greatest impacts.

Remember, Ananias was obedient to pray for Saul that he may receive his sight and the Holy Spirit. Saul became the great apostle Paul. We don't hear anything about Ananias before or after this, but that single act of obedience set a trajectory in the body of Christ that would last through the ages. Despise not the day of small or insignificant things (see Zechariah 4:10). God loves doing His greatest works through otherwise unnoticeable people.

Chapter Three
Group Discussion Questions

1. In his teaching on Daniel 2, Rick highlights the crumbling of the kingdoms of the world and the advancement of the kingdom of God. In what ways can we currently discern the kingdoms of this world crumbling? In what ways can we see the kingdom of God advancing? How do these two trends work together?

2. The influence of the kingdom of God on Russia started with leaders who sowed "little seeds" that grew to have a great impact. Identify one sphere of influence you have at home, at work, or elsewhere where the Lord can use you in greater ways. Ask the Lord for a "little seed" strategy to impact this sphere of influence for kingdom of heaven advancement.

Making "Sheep Nations" in His Kingdom

4

Signs of the next great awakening breaking out are becoming more numerous and more exciting. A second revival has broken out at Asbury University in Wilmore, Kentucky, fifty years after the last one. It quickly received international attention. By the end of the first day, busloads of students from other colleges and universities started arriving, and within a few days, they were coming from all over the world.

Revivals were a big part of America's First and Second Awakenings and, understandably, gather much attention. However, they are not the main purpose of an awakening. Revivals and movements are like the igniters and carriers of the work of the Holy Spirit, which is why they are often referred to as "waves of the Spirit." They are important, but an awakening is more like a rising tide than a wave.

A wave can lift many for a short time, but a rising tide can lift everyone for a much longer time. There have been multitudes of revivals and movements in the church age, but only two Great Awakenings. Revivals are short lived, as most are measured in weeks or a few in months. A few have lasted more than a year, like the recent Brownsville Revival in Pensacola, Florida. Awakenings last decades and are deeper and wider. They don't just bring transformation to churches but to entire nations. The Lord uses both because we need both.

I have studied church history for more than a half century, and I cannot recall hearing any teachings on "sheep" and "goat" nations until the last two decades. This is clearly biblical, but why has it not been emphasized before now? Because *now* is the time.

Only in the last few decades has there been this emphasis on the Great Commission to "make disciples of all nations," not just individuals. The details of what this looks like are now being worked out, and we are already seeing a diversity of methods being applied and working. Isn't that how the Lord moved in the past? He gave us directions, then left room for us to continually seek Him for the details, which are as diverse and creative as the rest of His works. The reason for such diversity is the diversity of nations He has made.

Nations were certainly impacted by the early church, and over time, most Western nations claimed to be "Christian nations." Though they may not have seemed like "Christian nations," they remained so because of their righteousness and justice, which are the foundations of the Lord's throne. At least they trended toward God and His ways, but it took them a long time to recognize the importance of personal salvation, discipleship, and devotion to Scripture rather than devotion to dogma. When this happened, the Reformation was born, with an even greater transformation of cultures and nations.

The Reformation was dramatic and shook most of the world. It did much to establish a devotion to sound biblical doctrine, which was desperately needed at the time and is still desperately needed in our time. Many could quote Scripture and doctrine, but with a few exceptions, not many lived them. As Spurgeon once lamented, "I can find ten more who will die for the Bible for every one who will actually read it." This continues to be a problem.

Throughout Scripture and history, there has always been a remnant, usually about ten percent, or a tithe, who walked in the truth, while most others just celebrated it. We should not be discouraged by this but rather rejoice, because only two percent of those who are passionate can radically change society. Ten percent can radically and profoundly change a civilization.

Leaven is a metaphor in Scripture for both good and evil. Good and evil are like leaven, because a tiny bit can change the nature of a large lump of dough. A few who are devoted to personal discipleship can be a mighty force for change in a nation.

Thus, the healthiest and most transformative moves of God are those that maintain an emphasis on personal discipleship and discipling nations. We must do both to have the greatest results. No matter how large or spectacular a revival is, it cannot be sustained without individuals who are intently focused on growing in the Lord. Those are the ones who keep the fires of revivals and awakenings burning.

We are now living in the time the Lord has saved for His best wine. As the angel told Daniel to seal up the prophecy until the end, it appears the end of the age is now upon us, and these prophecies are now being unsealed. We are also told in several biblical prophecies that His glory will be revealed at the end, which will cause the nations to turn to Him (see Isaiah 60:1-5). This is the greatest and most exciting time to be alive. Let us treasure this opportunity by resolving to make the most of it and by doing all for Him and for the sake of His gospel.

It is also clear that the previously "sealed" revelation is now being revealed because those who live at the end of the age will need it. That is why we are told in Joel 2 and Acts 2: **"In the last days"** the Lord will pour out of His Spirit, and there will be dreams, visions, and prophecy on the old and young, male and female, which includes everyone. The reason for this end-time prophetic revelation of dreams, visions, and prophecy is to have specific guidance for this revelation.

How does this all relate to this new emphasis on discipling nations and "sheep" and "goat" nations? In the Lord's parable of the sheep and goats, He explains that when He returns in His glory, the nations will be brought before Him at the judgment and divided into sheep and goats. The "sheep" nations will be invited into His kingdom; the "goat" nations will be assigned the same judgment as the devil and his followers. This is important because this emphasis has been reserved for our time.

This parable also teaches the important principle of treating the least of the Lord's people as we would treat Him. However, only recently have Christians realized this was spoken of nations, not just individuals. Now we see movements focused on helping nations become "sheep nations," so those nations can enter His kingdom. Again, this is important because now is the time for this to happen.

Since the beginning of the Reformation, we have learned the truth that salvation is personal, each one must be born again to enter the kingdom, and we are saved not because we are a citizen of a "Christian nation" or a church member. This greatly helped recover our individual values and gave greater emphasis to personal discipleship. This also contributed, nearly accidentally, to the birth of modern democracy. In fact, reformer John Calvin has been credited as "the father of modern democracy."

So, this emphasis on the value of individuals has impacted nations. As these truths were applied to nations, they had a profound impact on the advancement of civilization. However, this new teaching on sheep and goat nations is bringing a whole new level of emphasis on corporate redemption and the salvation of nations.

Much good has come from this, but also conflict, which is to be expected whenever great new emphases are introduced. Every new or rediscovered teaching that has impacted the body of Christ in major ways has been carried to unhealthy extremes by some. Is this one of

MAKING "SHEEP NATIONS" IN HIS KINGDOM

them? If so, how can we keep this important truth on a path that leads to life and not confusion?

The realization that the "sheep" and "goats" in the Lord's parable is about nations brought understanding to how the Great Commission can "make disciples of all nations," not just individuals. This realization has led to an even deeper realization of the importance of being salt and light to the nations in which God has placed us, which has already borne much good fruit, but there is more!

Just as every doctrine can get off-centered, every form of discipleship—whether for individuals or for nations—can get off-centered. To stay balanced, we must not forget to disciple individuals while we focus on nations, and we must not forget the nations as we disciple individuals.

Like every great principle and teaching of the faith with dual applications, we can expect some to get off centered in their application, overemphasizing some aspects without counterbalancing the truth. If we overemphasize the personal, we will not reach the world as we should. If we overemphasize the world, we will not grow as individuals.

The path of life is nearly always in the balance between two extremes. To keep from becoming off centered, we must recognize all biblical teachings. As Psalm 119:160 declares, **"The sum of Thy word is true."** Many extremes and heresies have resulted from overemphasizing one biblical teaching without considering other biblical teachings.

For example, we have the biblical teaching of living one day at a time and living with an eternal perspective. The path of a healthy, Christian life requires both. Emphasizing one without the other makes us unbalanced and unstable.

Another example is in the apostle Paul's exhortation to consider **"the kindness and the severity of God" (see Romans 11:22).** Those who see only the Lord's kindness without His severity are deceived. He is both. To see and relate to Him as He is, we must keep both in proper balance. One major reason for the weakness of Christianity in our time is the overemphasis on the Lord's kindness, grace, and mercy without understanding His wrath and judgments. Both are major Bible themes.

Again, many important biblical truths for which we are called to live are dualistic in nature. We must see and apply both to stay on the path of life. They are not contradictory but counterbalancing. The healthiest, most fruitful Christians are those who see both, do both, and maintain balance.

When I was a young Christian, I felt the Great Commission had been changed from "making disciples" to making converts, which diluted the power of the gospel. I have not changed my opinion on this. Helping each new convert become a disciple according to Jesus' definition is radical and crucial to living a truly victorious Christian life. It is also crucial to being a Christian who can impact our world. How can we disciple nations if we ourselves are not true disciples?

A true mark of maturity is seeing and applying both counterbalancing truths. One great hope for these extraordinary revivals and moves of God now emerging is that God has a remnant who has not wasted their time of relative spiritual inactivity to grow personally and have become both deep wells and deep rivers of truth. They are never the majority, but they don't need to be to bring clarity and definition and keep what is now unfolding on course, so it completes the work for which the Lord sent it.

CHAPTER FOUR
GROUP DISCUSSION QUESTIONS

1. Have you ever been part of a revival? Describe what happened, what the Lord did, and how it impacted you.

2. Rick asserts that we are on the brink of a major move of God in the nations and that effective discipleship is the best way to advance the kingdom when God moves. What are you currently doing to make disciples? How can you prepare to effectively disciple more people?

3. What can each of us do individually to disciple our nation more effectively? What can we do corporately as the body of Christ to disciple our nation more effectively?

TRAINING TO REIGN IN HIS KINGDOM

5

God's kingdom is where God reigns. He does not need our input or participation, but He desires it. We can be assured if Jesus had remained on the earth after His resurrection and had personally led the emerging church, things would have gone much better. However, He commissioned His apostles to do this with His help through the Holy Spirit.

What did the three thousand who gave their lives to the Lord on the day of Pentecost think of the apostles' leadership? Weren't these apostles the same ones who had just denied the Lord and scattered during His trial and execution? They could not trust these men, but they could trust the Holy Spirit who was in them. Likewise, the Lord's trust was not in these men, but in the Holy Spirit who was in them.

The point is, the Lord could do everything He has delegated to us much better if He did it Himself. The Lord knew that nothing done in this age would be done perfectly, but He was not looking for perfection as much as participation. This age is for the calling and training of those who will reign with Him in the coming age.

A second point is, the Lord does not and will not have perfect representatives on earth in this age. In Scripture and throughout history, those who accomplished the greatest things for God also made the biggest mistakes. We all have flaws and weaknesses because we are "earthen vessels." That our Lord would trust His glory and authority to earthen vessels is one of the greatest marvels.

Since such great patience has been shown to us, should we not show the same patience toward one another? There is no perfect church or perfect people anywhere on earth, and there will not be in this age. There are some extraordinary churches and exceptional leaders and teachers living in these times, and even greater ones are coming. Yet there are more false shepherds, false teachers, and false prophets than ever, and they have led the church into perhaps its weakest state. So, where is the church heading?

It will become a church "without spot or blemish." How can this be when it looks like the opposite is happening? Never forget that the greatest prophets and leaders always arise in the darkest of times. The greatest revivals have always come when God's people fell into the worst apostasies. Just fifty days after the worst failures of the first-century apostles, the day of Pentecost came, and the greatest move of God began.

Never lose hope in the Lord's church, because that is losing hope in the Lord. He promised to build His church, and He promised His church would become His worthy bride. It may take more faith to believe this now when things look grim, but perhaps that is why He allows us to get to this state. True faith grows when we are tested and yet do not shrink back or give up.

In fact, the worse the church gets, the more resolved we should be to grow in faith and do what He said. Just know that the worse shape the church is in, the greater the miracles we will experience.

Yes, the Lord will rule with a "rod of iron" when He returns, which will require, at least for a time, the world to fall into deep darkness and into the greatest time of trouble known to man. Still, we have His Word that we will ultimately see **"the restoration of all things" (see Acts 3:21).** Everything lost in the Fall will be recovered.

Man will be restored to the authority he was given in the garden and will be given rule over all the earth again. Only this time, we will have hopefully learned our lesson for all eternity—to never try anything without God.

God is the Supreme Delegator. He gave Adam authority over all the earth, over every living creature on the earth, in the air, and under the sea. He did all this knowing that Adam would fall, and that all mankind and creation would fall with him and end up in this state. His response was not to destroy us but to implement a plan for our complete restoration and a "new creation" which would end up greater than the original.

The Lord does not want to rule *over* us so much as He wants to rule *with* us. For a time, He may be strict, but always with the goal of us doing right because our hearts are right and because we want to. Still, the Lord knows doing things with us will never be as perfect as if He had done them alone. However, His main goal right now is not perfect works, but perfecting those He has called to rule and reign with Him.

This entire age has been about Him finding those who could rule and reign with Him, so He can restore mankind and the earth. Thus, if we are to be restored to His image and nature, we must have a heart for restoration.

Despite all the evil and rebellion man has lashed against God, He will never leave us nor forsake us. If we are being restored to His nature, we must also refuse to give up on the fallen, whether individuals or nations. As we are told repeatedly in Scripture, after the world has fallen into deep darkness, the nations will turn to Him.

The Lord can be strict and authoritarian when necessary, but His overriding purpose for us is to mature to the point that He can relate to us as friends, brothers, and sisters. After all, He originally created mankind for fellowship.

One important element for having a healthy walk with God is to know the timing and purpose for each stage of growth in Him. Just as parents give their children more freedom and authority as they mature, our Father does the same with us. How can we know which level of maturity we are in, and how much authority God has delegated to us? This is addressed in II Corinthians 13:5:

"Test yourselves to see if you are in the faith; examine yourselves! Or do you not recognize this about yourselves, that Jesus Christ is in you—unless indeed you fail the test?"

Since "all authority" has been given to Christ, we only have spiritual authority to the degree we abide in the King. Spiritual authority is not gained through knowledge but through our union with Him. How can we test ourselves to see whether we are in the faith according to this mandate?

I have asked many Christians this very question, and so far, have only received blank stares. It is true that we are told in several places that God is evaluating us, but that does not negate these instructions from the Lord to test ourselves. Why do we need to test ourselves if God does?

After the Fall, when the Lord asked Adam where he was, He was not seeking information. God is omniscient and knows all things. He was trying to get Adam to evaluate where he was. He is still doing this. His tests are for our sake, not His. He knows very well where we are, yet few Christians do. That is why we are so weak.

Self-evaluation is unpopular with some, and overly popular with others. If we become overly self-focused, we can fall into the black hole of self-centeredness. Still, self-evaluation is a requirement for success in any field, but none is more important than our Christian walk. Using biblical wisdom for this can help us have great confidence in our maturity level, as well as know our next steps.

As a professional pilot, I was tested every six months for each commercial aircraft I was qualified to fly. Most pilots become qualified in one, or at the most two, types of aircraft. However, because the air charter service I owned had a diverse fleet, I became qualified in more than half a dozen types of aircraft. Consequently, I was constantly preparing for the next test ride. I would not recommend this to anyone. However, my flying proficiency attained a level I could never have achieved without that much testing.

I was committed to being the best pilot I could be, so I embraced the challenge to constantly improve myself through these tests. They were a sure measure of my proficiency. More importantly, the challenges I was put through during these tests made actual emergencies seem relatively easy. I could handle each with little stress. Keeping calm in any emergency when flying is of utmost importance.

Once, I flew into a storm which I thought would end my life and take my aircraft beyond its limits and beyond our limits to survive. I cried out to the Lord to either calm the storm or somehow get me through it. Otherwise, I was coming home to see Him soon! Then I clearly heard Him say above all the clamor from the storm, "Your training was My grace to get you through this storm." Since I was in a squall line of storms, the rain was so heavy, my radar was useless to show me the way out. I remained in extreme turbulence for another twenty minutes, far beyond what most pilots or aircraft can handle. Obviously, I did survive, but without a doubt, I could not have done so without the intense training and testing I had received.

Never waste a trial. The Lord does not tempt us, but several times in Scripture, it does say He tests us. These tests are not for His sake but ours. I faced a few other serious emergencies as a pilot but never panicked. All that testing was, no doubt, the reason. Panic is a major cause of plane crashes and a major reason why many Christians make hasty, foolish decisions in crises and shipwreck their faith.

The Lord said, **"In the world, you will have tribulation" (see John 16:33).** That means, no one can escape it. So why not embrace the challenge and be determined to use these opportunities? James wrote, **"Consider it all joy...when you encounter various trials, knowing that the testing of your faith produces endurance" (see James 1:2).** When I endured the emergence of that storm, which was beyond what many would consider possible, it was because of the tough training and testing I endured.

No trial is arbitrary. The devil cannot get in potshots when the Lord is not looking. The Lord may not be doing these things to us, but He does allow them for our good. As we enter these times at the end of this age, when the greatest tribulation the world has known is unfolding, those who are prepared, having embraced His training, will never lose their peace or joy. Instead of being overcome by tribulation, we can be the overcomers the world looks to for hope.

We can do this by trusting in Him who called us to live in these times, and by knowing He will never allow us to be tempted or tested beyond our limits. No one passes God's tests with a perfect score, but in Him, even our failures work for our good. As we are told in Proverbs 24:16, **"For a righteous man falls seven times, and rises again."** God's definition of a righteous man is not one who never falls but one who keeps getting back up. Never quit!

CHAPTER FIVE
GROUP DISCUSSION QUESTIONS

1. Rick gives an example from the day of Pentecost to illustrate how God can use imperfect people to advance His kingdom. Describe a time when God used you in a powerful way despite your own inadequacies or weaknesses.

2. Rick points out the spiritual value of our trials in this chapter. What is the best way to respond to difficult trials in our lives? What mindsets should we develop concerning our trials?

3. Many people face difficult trials in church life. How does a heart of restoration and a focus on the Lord guard our hearts against the perils of bitterness, resentment, or negativity towards others in the body of Christ?

PREPARING THE WAY FOR HIS KINGDOM

6

One steady factor in these times is continuous crises breaking out. There seems to be at least one new crisis every week. They are becoming both more intense and more frequent. This is how "birth pangs" or contractions come upon a woman in labor. That is the metaphor both the Lord and the early church apostles used to describe how troubles would come upon the world at the end of the age. This is what we are now witnessing, and we must understand this to navigate through them.

The signs of the end of this age are signs of the imminent birth of the age to come. This is when the Lord returns to establish His kingdom on earth. To prepare the way for His kingdom, everything that can be shaken will be shaken, so He can build upon what cannot be shaken.

The prophetic signs given to us in Scripture are spiritual road signs. They let us know where we are and where we are heading. If we pay attention to them, we will realize when and where we made a wrong turn and started heading somewhere we did not want to go. These road signs can be used personally, for the body of Christ, or for nations. Through them, we can also see the timing for what is now unfolding.

Everyone can see the signs, but they may not know what they are or relate them to biblical prophecies. Economists tend to interpret these signs by how they affect the economy. Politicians evaluate them by their effects on politics. This can be useful knowledge, but the most important evaluation is what they mean in relation to the end of this age and the coming kingdom of God.

Earth's economies will be replaced by God's economy, built on His ways of love, generosity, and everyone seeking to do good for one another. Human politics will be replaced by a leadership of true shepherds who serve with the Lord's heart and wisdom, not selfish ambition. We are not there yet, and we have some great challenges to go through before we arrive. However, these challenges are for us to use to help prepare the way for His coming. Never lose sight of how the things that are happening are leading us to the birth of a new age—the kingdom of God coming to earth. That is our main purpose for being here and must remain the focus of our lives. This is also the primary lens we must look through to do our jobs and remain on the path of life.

Every major crisis is basically the result of mankind thinking we can run this world without God. This great time of trouble will teach us that we must never try to do that again. He is allowing us to see the fruit of this folly and using it to clear the land for His coming kingdom, in which all things will be restored from the consequences of man trying to rule the earth without Him.

However, He does not want to rule the world without us, so He is allowing us to learn all we need to rule with Him in the age to come. If we think we cannot use most of what we learn in this life, that is correct; it is *not* for this life. This does not mean we cannot use any of it. We are here to help nations become "sheep nations," so when He comes and divides the nations into sheep and goats, we can help prepare them for the coming transition.

Though we still have a ways to go, we are not here as observers. We need to learn all we can from this experience to become workers helping prepare the way for the Lord.

To be on solid ground economically in these times, we must build our lives on the clear biblical principles of economics and resist following the shaky ways of this world, which are now beginning to crumble. Still, the main reason for us to prosper is not to live well, but to help prepare the way for the Lord.

According to Psalm 89:14, God's kingdom is built on the two pillars of righteousness and justice. These are based on God's definitions of righteousness and justice, which He has given us throughout the Scriptures. It has been estimated that between one third and one half of the biblical teachings on righteousness have to do with stewardship. Being a steward of God's garden was one of the first commands given to man. How are we doing with this?

A few years ago, a study was done on world debt in relation to assets. The conclusion was that world debt was already several times the value of all the assets in the world combined. Since then, the difference between them has grown dramatically. How will this debt ever be repaid if it is several times the value of all assets on earth?

God established the principle of Jubilee thousands of years ago. Even Israel did not apply it, which is a major reason why God allowed them to go into captivity. It will be applied in the coming kingdom, and it will be done rightly and justly.

We must consider the things that are shaking in our economy now in light of basic biblical principles for doing what is right and just economically. When we look at economics, we don't want to just look for what works or make us successful, but what is right and just. We need to start living by the principles of His kingdom now, even when they are inconvenient or costly.

A few years ago, a leftist politician said, "You never want a serious crisis to go to waste." I have heard this is an evil statement, but it is also a biblical concept. It is a basic Marxist tactic to use every crisis to push the Marxist agenda, but it was first given to God's people to be used for good. Jesus said, **"the children of this world are wiser than the children of the kingdom" (see Luke 16:8).** We must learn to use every crisis as an opportunity for good. This is what the apostle Paul meant when he said in Acts 14:22, **"Through many tribulations we must enter the kingdom."** Tribulations are doorways to the kingdom, and we must learn to recognize and enter through them.

Crises are some of the best teaching moments, and we must not allow those with evil intent to use them without challenge. Our challenge is to counter the enemy's intent with a hope and clarity that those in this "present evil age" cannot match.

The recent banking crisis that began with the failure of the Silicon Valley Bank (SVB) is a sign of the times.

Knowing what caused this and how it can be fixed without causing even more problems is crucial. This story contains a major revelation of what will ultimately cause our entire economy to collapse if we do not correct what we are doing.

A major problem that surfaced as a cause of the SVB failure was its management style, which lacked serious discipline and competence. It was said perhaps no one on the board of this bank understood much about banking. This was quickly traced to the SVB culture of pursuing "wokeness" over competence. This "management style" is now the prevailing force in virtually every major industry and field of power and influence power, including our own government.

This culture of wild, out-of-control spending by the federal government to shape culture instead of fulfilling its basic constitutional purpose has affected our economics and the nation in general. If not corrected soon, this will lead to an ultimate collapse.

One example of this is our current U.S. Transportation Secretary, Pete Buttigieg. He recently indicated that diversity is more important than safety. Could there be any greater disconnect from reality or from the purpose of government than this? If safety and efficiency are not our top priorities, we will have many more catastrophes. Secretary Buttigieg's response to the recent airline mishaps and train wrecks has been to not respond. He is obviously in way over his head. His response to the supply chain crisis was to hire new interns! It is madness to have such a level of administrative incompetence in the most powerful nation on earth. It would be a bit more comforting if Buttigieg was an extreme case, yet he is indicative of just about every other department in our government.

There will be more chips to fall in banking and every other sector. As regulators began to investigate the failure of SVB, it was quickly discovered the bank had given tens of millions to Black Lives Matter and other leftist organizations. This has been the case with many other banks, including some of the largest banks. Some banks have not drunk this wokeness poison and are devoted to sound banking policies and management, but they are becoming increasingly rare because of the political weaponization of our government. Our republic cannot survive this much longer.

Our government's response to SVB's collapse was to have the FDIC cover all deposits. Though this may temporarily restore confidence in the banking system, it is likely the worst thing they could have done. Now, the

American taxpayers are on the hook for such insane practices. Thus, without our consent, we and our children are paying for their incomprehensibly bad decisions, while those responsible pay nothing for their folly with little or no incentive to change.

Meanwhile, a recent in-depth study has revealed a massive pushback by an increasing majority of Americans to this woke, authoritarian agenda and the growing lack of trust multiplies with each new revelation of the current madness in our government.

The degrading of our military is another perfect example in which an increasingly disproportionate amount of time and resources are being spent on replacing military readiness with diversity training. The results are frightening. Promotions are now based on political compliance rather than competence. The result is what the world witnessed in the recent Afghanistan withdrawal. This has since been called the most chaotic and embarrassing debacle in U.S. military history in which 80 billion dollars in advanced weaponry and resources were left in the hands of our enemies to be used against us.

Seeing this, our enemies have begun a full-court press against our interests around the world. We are now enduring shocking indignities like Communist Chinese spy balloons flying over our country surveilling our military bases and communication systems, and having American military aircraft being taken out in international airspace. Such embarrassments give our enemies a strategic advantage in their dealings not only with us but with our allies and the rest of the world. Such degrading of our military has happened shockingly fast. The bully spirit is winning, but bullies are never satisfied, which will ultimately force a confrontation for which our leaders and military are not ready.

We currently have serious structural problems throughout our government, and this has crept into nearly every economic sector. In the 2008 "Great Recession," we came as close as ever to an entire meltdown of our economy. Word came out the weekend after the SVB collapse that we again came close to an economic meltdown. How did we avoid this? Politicians claim credit, but it was the One watching over us who said it was not yet time.

We now have people in the most powerful positions in the world who do not know what they are doing. If that's not bad enough, investigations have revealed a collusion between our president, his family members, and the Chinese Communist Party involving payments of millions of dollars. This is deeply troubling.

All this has one common cause—a crisis of leadership. This crisis is not only in government, but also in business, education, media, and the church. As we read in Isaiah 5:20, immature, capricious leadership is the first judgment of God that comes upon any **"who call evil good, and good evil."** Our country and much of the world is now there, and this vacuum of leadership is the result.

This may all seem overwhelming, and it is. It is beyond human remedy, but we serve a God with Whom nothing is impossible. In fact, He has always done His best work when things were beyond our ability to fix. The first and most important remedy is that we, as a nation, must turn back to God, after having asked Him to leave our country and having told Him we want nothing to do with Him. America is now even punishing those who use His name except to curse or blame God for its problems.

We must begin by repenting personally. He warned us if we deny Him before men, He will deny us before the Father and His angels (see Matthew 10:33). In Revelation, the first to get thrown in the lake of fire, which is the second and final death, are the cowards (see

Revelation 21:8). There can be no place for cowardice among true followers of Christ.

Cowardice only proves we are *not* true followers but imposters. However, as Peter learned after denying the Lord three times in one night, there is mercy for the repentant. His repentance was proven real by how he became the boldest witness. Regardless of how we have failed to stand up for our Lord and His truth, we too can repent and find mercy and grace to become bold witnesses. We must be bold to be the salt and light we were called to be.

The Lord is and always has been our only hope.

Chapter Six
Group Discussion Questions

1. Read Matthew 24 together. Which signs were fulfilled when the temple was destroyed in AD 70? Which signs are being fulfilled right now? Which signs have not yet come to pass?

2. In a time of increasing economic instability, how can we be sure that our finances are built on a strong foundation? What are you doing to prepare for increasing financial turmoil right now?

3. The world faces a leadership crisis. What is one historical or contemporary leader that you admire or that God has used? What character traits of this leader can you emulate to help advance God's kingdom on the earth?

Looking for the Signs of His Kingdom

7

It seems the signs of the coming kingdom are increasing faster and faster. The day is surely near when this will no longer be a message about the coming kingdom of God but the announcement, "It is upon us!" This is the seventh and last trumpet to be sounded in Revelation, which is "Our God reigns!"

Of course, "every eye will see Him," so we won't need an announcement, but this will be a proclamation of sheer joy since it has finally come. As the times become more intense, everything we say and do will have greater significance, as will our faith. Faith is the currency of the kingdom, so just as the currency of any nation that ascends increases in value, so will our faith.

When asked about the signs of the end of the age, most of what the Lord discussed were troubles on the earth. He said it will be the greatest time of trouble the world has ever known. One major thing we can do now to prepare for this is to resolve to trust in the Lord and His coming kingdom more than we fear anything the world can do to us. Through this trust, we can build an unconquerable fortress for ourselves, our loved ones, and others.

As the signs of His coming kingdom increase, let's focus our attention on the most important sign—His presence. Even the chaos increasing in civilization is a sign of His presence: **"the mountains will melt like wax at the presence of the Lord" (see Psalm 97:5).** Mountains are symbols of governments in Scripture, and today we are seeing even the most strong and stable governments melt like wax. This not only testifies to the instability of the greatest works of men but is also a sign of His growing presence.

"And His voice shook the earth then, but now He has promised, saying, 'Yet once more I will shake not only the earth, but also the heaven.'

"This expression, 'Yet once more,' denotes the removing of those things which can be shaken, as of created things, so that those things which cannot be shaken may remain.

"Therefore, since we receive a kingdom which cannot be shaken, let us show gratitude, by which we may offer to God an acceptable service with reverence and awe" (Hebrews 12:26-28).

This shaking the whole earth is beginning to experience is the Lord clearing the land for what He is about to build—a kingdom that *cannot* be shaken. That which has already been built on this solid foundation will not be lost but will become part of the highway we must build to prepare for the Lord (see Isaiah 40:3). So, now that everything is shaking, let's look to stand upon what is not being shaken.

If anything in the natural world was stable, it would be the laws of physics, but now even these are being shaken. With each new discovery, it is now apparent that these laws are and were at best only partially right. As we are told in I Corinthians 13:9, **"we know in part,"** and this is proving true in all things.

Einstein's theory of relativity first proposed the existence of black holes, yet he never believed they existed because they so profoundly violated the laws of physics they "knew" at the time. Evidently, the laws of physics are not as comprehensive as we thought.

Stephen Hawking wrote the equations that "proved" the existence of black holes and helped open the doors to quantum physics and mechanics. Many of those theories have since been mostly proven, but we still cannot figure out how they connect to other physical laws.

Then, the date and age of the physical universe seemed overwhelmingly confirmed, until James Webb's telescope peered close to what we thought was the "big bang," or the beginning of the universe. Expecting to see stars beginning to form, we instead saw mature galaxies. Of course, this threw a big wrench in our understanding of astronomy and physics.

In short, we tend to think we know more than we do. Even our most sure "laws" are constantly being challenged by new discoveries. However, there is one constant every new scientific discovery confirms—the Word of God. His sure Word has never changed and never will (see II Peter 1:19 KJV). It is a rock that has never been shaken.

So, while everything else is being shaken, why not put more trust in His Word? His Word is absolute, and it determined all the other laws we are still pondering. The wise will resolve every day to strengthen their knowledge and grow their faith in God's Word.

The Word commands us to "cultivate" our faith (see Psalm 37:3). Cultivation involves preparing soil, providing water, weeding, and watching until fruit is borne. Do we care enough about the words He has given to us to do this?

In Matthew 24, the disciples asked Jesus three questions which resulted in His discourse about the end of this age. Jesus had just told them about the coming destruction of Jerusalem and the temple, so their first question was, **"When will these things happen?" (see Matthew 24:3)**

Their next question was, **"What will be the sign of Your coming?" (see Matthew 24:3)** The Greek word translated "coming" here is *parousia*, which means "presence." To be present is very different from coming. A different Greek word for "coming" is used elsewhere concerning His second coming, like in Matthew 16:28: **"till they see the Son of Man coming in His kingdom."** This word is *erchomai*. So, when the disciples asked about the sign of His "presence," this clearly preceded His coming. Christ's second coming will be the ultimate event at the end of the age, which is why they asked in Matthew 24:3, **"What will be the sign ... of the end of the age?"**

To distinguish between these two Greek words in the New Testament could modify many people's eschatology, or theology of the end times, because they obviously speak of two distinct events. If we could read the New Testament in Greek, uncluttered by our eschatology, we could see that the presence of the Lord will come on the world for a time, and that this will precede the Lord's second coming.

His *parousia*, or presence, is to prepare the way for the Lord's coming. This will include the time of the harvest, the reaping of the earth, and the collapse of man's kingdoms (see Daniel 2). This is the time we are now entering.

Most biblical prophecies concerning His *parousia* do not set a specific time but show an unfolding over time. His *erchomai*, however, is set for a specific time. This distinction seemed to be understood by His disciples when they asked Him the three questions.

Not distinguishing the time of His presence from His coming has confused many people. His *parousia* is not, nor does it supplant, His literal second coming. Instead, it is a special time to prepare the way for Him to come and to establish His kingdom on the earth.

Since the disciples asked these three questions at the same time, many throughout the ages assumed they were asking the same question. They were not. Likewise, some wrongly assumed this entire discourse was about the destruction of Israel and the dispersion of the Jewish people, which occurred in AD 70. It clearly was not.

Some of this confusion occurred because this was the end of the age of the Jews and the beginning of the "times of the Gentiles." For nearly two thousand years, the Lord had dealt nearly exclusively with the Jewish people. Since then, the Lord has dealt mostly with the Gentiles. The end of the time of the Gentiles will not usher in another time of the Jews, but rather the Jews and Gentiles coming together **"into one new man" (see Ephesians 2:15).**

In Romans 9-11, Paul made clear some issues about the relationship between Jews and Gentiles which, if understood, will eliminate much confusion. The Jews are the natural seed of Abraham. The Gentiles are the spiritual seed of Abraham who were grafted into this tree when the Jews were seemingly cut off. These "wild" branches did not displace the natural branches. At the right time, the "natural branches" will be grafted back in, and the two will become one.

Some of the contradictions in eschatology can also be eliminated by an understanding of Romans 9-11. However, like other truths, this can only come by revelation of the Holy Spirit. In God's wisdom, He seemed to conceal this until it was almost time for it to happen. He did the same with the beginning of "the time of the Gentiles." The Lord told His disciples the gospel would be preached to the Gentiles, and this was clear in biblical prophecies, but they could not understand it until Peter had the vision and went to Cornelius' house.

Similarly, today, most of the natural seed, even if they believe in Jesus as their Messiah, only see the earthly Jerusalem, and fail to comprehend the New Jerusalem coming down from heaven. Likewise, most Christians only see the New Jerusalem without seeing the purpose of God for the natural seed or natural Jerusalem. However, we expect this will soon change. Neither can fully understand God's purposes without seeing both the natural and spiritual seeds.

Abraham's seed is both earthly and heavenly, which is why the Lord compared it to the sand on the seashore and the stars in the heavens. God loves the earthly and physical and the heavenly and spiritual. He made man to be a bridge between the two, which will be fulfilled when the natural and spiritual seeds of Abraham are made into "one new man," which will reveal what the new creation will be like.

God made the natural and spiritual realms to be vitally connected. When His kingdom comes, mankind will be restored to how they were created before the Fall. Man was created to have fellowship with God, who is Spirit. Therefore, man has a great spiritual void which can only be filled by God. When our reconciliation with God becomes complete, the spiritual realm will become far more real to us. Of course, we keep growing spiritually until we become more at home in the spiritual realm, while we are still at home in the natural realm.

Paul made clear in Romans 9-11, the promises God made with the natural seed were not nullified but completed by the new covenant, just as Jesus came not to do away with but to fulfill the law. The law was the "tutor" to lead us to Christ. It brought the consciousness of sin. We cannot repent or be reconciled to God without knowing our sins and transgressions.

This important tutor taught us that walking by the law was beyond human ability and therefore could not make us righteous. This made us completely dependent on the cross and what Jesus did as our only hope of salvation from our sins. Thus, turning to Christ is compared to dying to the law and becoming married to Christ (see Romans 7:4). Likewise, returning to the law is considered spiritual adultery, because we are turning away from Christ, our righteousness, and returning to our former relationship under the law.

Jesus fulfilled the law and replaced all its commandments with two—love God and love your neighbor. If we do these two, we keep all the others because, if we love God, we will not worship idols, and if we love our neighbors, we will not envy, steal, kill, or otherwise do harm.

Our fallen human nature does not know how to love, so we can only love Him and others by abiding in Him. Since we depend on His Holy Spirit to love and do everything else we are called to do, we become more dependent on Him as we lose trust in our earthly, carnal nature. By this we are transformed from the earthly to the spiritual.

"In all wisdom and insight He made known to us the mystery of His will, according to His kind intention which He purposed in Him with a view to an administration suitable to the fullness of the times, that is, the summing up of all things in Christ, things in the heavens and things on the earth" (Ephesians 1:8-10). All things will be summed up in Christ, and the entire purpose of this age is for us to be conformed to His image, so we can be that bridge that brings others to Him for the same purpose.

Everything in the old covenant pointed to Christ; everything in the new covenant is fulfilled in Him. We are reconciled to God through Christ, and we live a life that is pleasing to Him by abiding in Christ, not in our own strength, wisdom, or perceived goodness.

We must also settle, once and for all, that there is no way to do this except through Jesus. To presume otherwise is the epitome of human arrogance. We cannot be more prideful than to reject God's provision for our redemption and reconciliation through His Son and the unfathomable price He paid, or to think we don't need His provision and can do this without Him.

When the natural seed of Abraham is grafted back in, it will be by their recognition of "the one whom they pierced." Those who are forgiven much for rejecting the One through whom all their promises were made, love much. Since the church cannot come into its fullness without this grafting in of the Jews, praying and looking for this should be a high priority of all believers.

Neither can we fully comprehend the biblical prophecies concerning the end of this age without understanding this joining together of Jews and Gentiles "into one new man." This can only happen when this ultimate racist barrier between Jews and Gentiles is overcome. This is essential for this bridge between the natural and spiritual to be completed, and why Paul said their acceptance would result in **"life from the dead"** (see

Romans 11:15). In other words, when this happens, resurrection is upon us, and the kingdom of God will come.

So, in identifying the signs of the end of this age, which are now unfolding, let us not forget that Israel is one of the major signs of the times. It is that "fig tree" the Lord said would sprout (see Joel 2:21-23; Matthew 24:32-33). Let us pray for the peace of Jerusalem and seek the salvation and fullness of their destiny, since our destiny is vitally linked to theirs.

The spiritual seed cannot see the destiny of the natural seed without being humble about their role, nor can the natural seed see the destiny of the spiritual seed without being humble about their role. Humility will be required on both sides, and since God gives grace to the humble, this will bring essential grace to both. Such ultimate grace will be needed for these times.

CHAPTER SEVEN
GROUP DISCUSSION QUESTIONS

1. Read I Thessalonians 4:13-18 together. What details of this description are most important to you? Why is it important to teach about the Lord's coming and look forward to it?

2. Today, many people put their trust in systems that are being severely shaken. What practical steps can we take to build our lives on the "kingdom that cannot be shaken"?

3. Take time to pray for the nation of Israel and for the Jewish people who are still scattered throughout the earth.

Approaching the King of Kings

8

Our ministry celebrates nearly every July as a sabbatical month. We shut down the ministry, including church services, to give ourselves to seeking God, spending time with families, and enjoying God's blessings in our own way. This has had a large impact on us, as each August we experience palpable renewed vision and energy throughout the ministry.

Each sabbatical, I try to find specific ways to learn about the Lord and His ways that I can apply to my life. For example, the Lord gives much attention to "days," such as **"Give us this day our daily bread" (Matthew 6:11)** and **"Today if you hear His voice, do not harden your hearts" (see Hebrews 3:15).** So, last year I spent the month trying to define the perfect day and seeking to live it. I still don't think I have lived the perfect day yet, but I have come close a few times. Still, just having this as a goal made the whole year better and brought more traction to my spiritual growth.

This approach may not work for everyone, but to break down something as big as spiritual maturity into smaller, achievable steps can bring significant changes to our lives. Few things in life are more fulfilling than knowing you are making progress, taking ground, or getting stronger and better. It's easy for bodybuilders to see results, but building up our inner person without defined markers can be a challenge.

Doing this has helped me become spiritually disciplined. However, there is one potential snare; it can make me more self-centered than God-centered. The goal of every Christian is to have "Christ in you, the hope of glory," not just be a better version of yourself. We are changed into His image, from glory to glory, by seeing *His* glory (see II Corinthians 3:18). Are we seeing His glory? One way to do this is by seeking to glorify Him and not ourselves.

What if we started each day resolving to see His glory by seeking to glorify Him? That would be the most important thing we could accomplish that day, so should this not be first on our daily to-do lists?

Speaking of lists, it has been said that no one becomes successful without learning how to make and use lists. Having been in leadership positions most of my life, I have learned that even the most brilliant and zealous people are undependable without this skill. There may be exceptions to this, but I have not seen any.

Personally, I have never had a good short-term memory. If I don't write things down, I am likely to forget them. The definition of carelessness is to care less. Isn't everything we do for the King important enough to at least write it down?

I have even learned to include things that are on my spiritual to-do list on my prayer list. If something is the will of God for my life, I pray for the wisdom and grace to do it and to do it well. What can be more important than to accomplish what the King has assigned to us?

If the most important thing in our lives is to love God, is there a way to measure when our love for God grows? This is—and should be—subjective, but what is subjective is difficult to define or measure. Has God increasingly become the focus of our lives? Is He the One we think about and long to be with? Our "first love" fills our minds and thoughts whenever possible. Is God our first love? Is our affection for Him growing?

One of the most serious warnings about the end of this age is in Matthew 24:12: **"Because lawlessness is increased, most people's love will grow cold."** He did not say the love of "many" but the love of "most" would grow cold. This word of the Son of God is sure, so we know most Christians will lose their love for Him. Is this not the worst thing that could happen to a Christian? If so, what can we do to prevent this from happening to most Christians in these times?

If we are not proactively guarding against what Jesus Himself warned, then we may be among those who will lose their love for Him in the last days if we have not already. But take courage; if you are reading this, you still care. Even if you have lost some of your affection for Him, you still have enough left to turn this around and recover what you have lost.

Still, to avoid the future jeopardy of losing our love for God, we must do more than just recover what we have lost. We must have a plan and goal to grow in our love for Him. To grow in any relationship requires investment, and our most valuable relational investment is our time. Do we allot time every day to seek the Lord? And is this our most valuable time, when we are most fresh and alert, or do we just give Him the leftovers?

Prayer is the primary scriptural way to seek the Lord. What is our prayer life like? Do we grow impatient for this time to end? For those we truly love, we are never glad when our time with them is up.

If our prayer lives are lifeless, we can make them better. However, don't try to begin at your end goal; take small steps first. The devil will try to make you feel guilty for not praying at least an hour a day, knowing this will frustrate you and make you dislike prayer. I encourage believers to begin by praying five minutes a day. Anyone can pray for five minutes. Then, instead of wanting your prayer time to end, after a few days, you'll be wishing your time was longer. Let your prayer time increase naturally. Aim for quality, not quantity.

Prayer lists can help our prayers stay focused. Log what you are praying for along with the answers. Prayer is not about logging time or boring repetition; it's about communication with the highest authority in the universe. He is the Highest One, but He also understands how clumsy we are and how we get better with practice. We also want to be effective in prayer, and that can be measured by the answers we receive to our prayers.

As we grow in our love for praying, we will grow in our love for the Lord. We will better understand how important it is to have times when we listen to Him, so we can pray according to His will. We will also learn how times of waiting upon the Lord can renew our strength and allow us to soar higher in the Spirit like eagles. Growing in prayer can be the best part of our day and bring the best out of our lives.

CHAPTER EIGHT
GROUP DISCUSSION QUESTIONS

1. Describe a "big goal" the Lord has put on your heart to accomplish. What simple daily steps can you take to help you reach this goal?

2. Rick recommended creating "spiritual to-do lists" to help us take action on the things the Lord is speaking to us. What are the top three things the Lord has laid on your heart to become the kind of person He has called you to be?

3. Share the top three things you have been praying about lately, then take turns agreeing with each other in prayer.

Pursuing, Knowing, and Loving the King

The Scriptures indicate that Jesus will come *to* His people and *in* them before He comes *for* them. We are told He will **"suddenly" (see Malachi 3:1)** come to His temple, which is now the body of Christ. What will it look like when the Lord is fully manifested *in* His people? We are told some of this in Ephesians 4:11-16. However, many details seem left out, so we can only dream and seek Him for their reality.

The early church in Jerusalem experienced this but not its fullness. The early church was the seed; the end of the age is the harvest when we can expect this to reach full maturity. Later we will go over the biblical prophecies that indicate how His glory will appear *in* His people at the end of the age, but for now let's look at the two most basic ways we can prepare to be part of this full manifestation. Both involve continuous expectation of His coming.

One key warning He gave is to be awake and watching for His appearing. This is repeated enough times in Scripture that it should be foremost in all our minds. How do we do this?

One analogy the Lord gave is to be waiting and watching for Him like a bride for her bridegroom. There are few things in this world as focused as a bride waiting for her bridegroom. As intense as this is in the weeks before that great day, as the days draw nearer, the focus and intensity only increase!

Likewise, our love and desire for Him should increase over time. If not, we have somehow drifted from the way. Jesus said eternal life was to know Him and the Father (see John 17:3). If we are not in hot pursuit of knowing Him, we are most certainly drifting from Him. He also warned that most people's love would grow cold (see Matthew 24:12). For our love to grow cold, we must first have loved Him. Yet we are told, "most" will lose their love for Him. Is there any tragedy in life worse than this?

If we are not intentional and persistent about pursuing, knowing, and loving Him as the main focus of our lives, we will lose it. God is love, so as we grow in our knowledge of Him, we can't help but love Him more. As that day nears for every bride, the anticipation grows until it becomes all consuming. Even the greatest storybook wedding is but a foretaste of our union with Christ. How can this day not become our greatest anticipation?

How can any distraction in this life overshadow this? Anything that can has become our focus. If we have experienced even a taste of "first love" with another person, then we know this person dominates our thoughts. Does He likewise dominate our thoughts, hopes, and vision? If not, we must review the reason for the hope that is in us and daily recount it (see I Peter 3:15).

Christians who keep their love for Him burning brighter and brighter as their expectation for His appearing likewise grows, but die without experiencing His coming, lose nothing. They will receive that for which they have faithfully waited and gain an unsurpassed richness and depth in this life. Keeping this hope for Him and what He will do when He returns foremost in our hearts not only ennobles our priorities, but also awakens us to what is happening around us and how we must become more engaged. Living with a growing love for the Lord is the best life we can live.

The second warning the Lord gave to keep us focused on His return is to let us know the day of the Lord will come like a thief in the night. The highest and most noble motive for expecting His return is our love for Him, but a second motive is fear for what we will lose if we do not keep expecting. We may consider this a shallow, less noble motive, yet it is one Jesus gave us because it helps us stay focused.

Those who say they care little for what they will receive only deceive themselves and others. It is not wrong to be motivated by what we will receive. The Lord would not give us such promises if they did not help us look forward to His appearance. Jesus went to the cross for the joy that was set before Him (see Hebrews 12:2). Love for Him is the higher motive, but He also shared many things about what we would receive for following Him because He knew this would help.

So, we should recount His promises, each of which are more valuable than any treasure in this world. They can both help us to stay awake and to expect His appearance. If we are not awake and looking forward to His appearing, and keeping our vessels full of oil, we could lose this most precious of all treasures.

The world is full of many traps and distractions, all meant to rob us of our inheritance in Christ. Those whose faith is more in Christ and His promises than in the things of this world will not succumb to them. Do we esteem Him and His purposes above all else, enough to focus on them for many years or for our entire lives? If we truly believe in Him and His promises, this is but a small requirement to be joined to the Creator Himself and to receive all He has promised to His faithful ones.

CHAPTER NINE
GROUP DISCUSSION QUESTIONS

1. Rick strongly recommends that we be intentional and persistent in our pursuit of intimacy with God. How can you put this recommendation to practice in your own life? What advice would you give to those who feel they are drifting away?

2. What can we do to increase our awareness of the Lord's presence in our midst? What can we do each day to open the door for Him to come in and fellowship with us?

3. Rick highlights the value of the Lord's promises in this chapter. Which promises of God are most treasured in your own life? Why?

Learning How to Approach the King 10

Knowing what will happen in our times is not nearly as important as knowing and being in the Lord's will for our lives. Knowing the Lord's will for our personal lives requires more than just knowing the Scriptures, though this is important. The Lord did not say, "I am going away but I will send a book to lead you into all truth." No, He said I will send you the Spirit of truth who will lead you into all truth and lead you to Me.

As Francis Frangipane used to say, "We are not called to follow a manual, but Emmanuel." Christianity is not about following a book but a Person. The Book He has given us is a great treasure and aid to knowing Him, but men have allowed their devotion to the Book of the Lord to eclipse their devotion to the Lord of the Book. If this is not kept in check, we can become modern Pharisees.

Still, most Christians are not devoted *enough* to the Book of the Lord. So, the answer is not to esteem the Bible less but more, and to maintain an even greater devotion to knowing and following the Lord.

I like to remind us of this several times a year in my *Word for the Week* and in *The MorningStar Journal* because we need constant reminders. But now I will discuss another factor I have not addressed that can also help us abide in the Lord. This is becoming increasingly rare in our times, yet it can greatly help us keep our lives on track —good manners.

Good manners is one primary way we show our care and respect for others. Having good manners is also a primary factor for success in our lives. I know of numerous cases in which people who applied for employment, who were less qualified, graduated from less impressive schools and were near the bottom of their classes were offered positions because they displayed good manners during their interviews.

This is so important in our lives. I spend a good deal of time in our monthly lunches with our high school seniors training them in how to conduct good interviews. Whether interviewing for a job or for higher education, good manners can set the course for the rest of our lives.

How to approach our King is also one of the most vitally important protocols we will ever learn. I have heard varying opinions on this, and they may all work, but this is only because of the graciousness of the Lord, not because we are doing it right. Why does this matter?

In my experience, the Lord is not nearly as formal or religious as we are. During some recent personal health challenges, I was amazed at how the King of kings, the Creator of the universe, would stay so close to me during my lowest times. I know He can do this for everyone at once, but it's not so much that He can, but that He does. He will go far beyond what even our closest human friends will do—yet He is the highest King!

My point is, I'm not trying to add formality to our relationship with God, but He did teach us to give honor to whom honor is due, and there is no one more deserving of honor than the Lord. We should seek any way we can to better honor Him, not because we have to but because we want to.

There are also biblical teachings and examples of how not observing protocols can be extremely costly. For example, not coming to His wedding party properly dressed can get us thrown into outer darkness (see Matthew 22:11-13). Perhaps we have never been taught how to dress appropriately for things like this, However, those who care will research such things because they care.

How we dress for a wedding shows our respect for the bride and groom and their families.

We may think society has become far less formal, and having never been a slave to fashion, I like this. However, is this heaven's perspective or just a reflection of what's happening on earth, most of which is no longer turning to what is true and right? Should we let the lowering of earthly standards affect our kingdom's standards?

Once, when having lunch with Derek Prince, he told me he rose up early every morning, showered, and put on his best suit before praying. I knew Derek well enough to know he did not share things like this without having a point to make. I also knew he was trying to highlight to me that I might be too informal in my approach to the Lord. I took this seriously. Though I still don't rise up and put on a suit before praying, I did start examining ways I might be too casual in my relationship with the Lord.

This was also something Leonard Ravenhill emphasized: Judas was familiar with the Lord, John was intimate. There's a difference and that difference can have consequences. When formality or protocol is required, I want to be the very best at it in showing respect for the Lord and His people. I don't *have* to do this, I *want* to. The Lord deserves this more than anyone.

John is known as "the disciple whom Jesus loved." Of course, the Lord loved all His disciples, but had a special affection for John and John with Him. Decades later, when John was on the Isle of Patmos, the only remaining apostle who had walked with the Lord longer than any other and had been the most intimate, when he saw Jesus in a vision, he fell to the ground like a dead man! (see Revelation 1:17). As close as John had been to the Lord, he never lost his awe and respect for who He was.

When I hear someone claim to have had a spiritual experience of heaven or with the Lord and His angels that make them seem frivolous and silly, I realize they're not talking about the Jesus I know or of the heaven I have experienced. I consider this not only spiritually unhealthy but also dangerous to promote a perspective of God, His angels, and His kingdom that makes people more like Judas than John.

Yet I'm glad the Lord is not stuffy or uptight. Otherwise, we would all be in serious trouble. We really can come to Him as we are. He is our Father and He delights in us wanting to come to Him as His children and climb up on His lap. However, with the Lord, or anyone deserving of honor, I want to do more than the required minimum to maintain my respect for who they are.

Since the Lord said how we treat even the least of His brothers is how we treat Him, how do we treat His people? When a friend becomes pushy or disrespectful to my staff, they quickly become a former friend. How they treat my staff is an indication of how they respect me, and since everyone on our staff is one of the Lord's children, I consider their disrespect for them as disrespect for the Lord and try to steer as far away from people like that as I can.

The Lord said if anyone tried to enter any other way than through the door, they are a thief who has come to steal and destroy. I have also learned that people who want to meet with me but do not want to follow the simple procedure I have for meetings are thieves who have come to steal one of my most precious possessions—time.

The simple procedure I have for setting up a meeting is to contact my assistant and request one. She will ask the purpose of the meeting so I can be prepared, and how much time is needed, so I can fit it into my schedule. Sadly, many people think they're so important that such rules don't apply to them. That's how a thief thinks. They're so proud they get offended when they're required to do as others. These are not people with whom I want to associate.

LEARNING HOW TO APPROACH THE KING

Many will protest that the Lord was always accessible to anyone who came to Him at any time. Really? They must have a different Bible than I have. In the Gospels we see how well Jesus was shielded by His disciples. True, some with extraordinary faith could penetrate that shield, but those were divine setups He was expecting because He only did what He saw His Father do.

Manners were developed as a way for us to show dignity and respect for one another. If we really take seriously the first and second commandments, to love the Lord above all, and to love others as we should, we will care enough to learn, teach, and to use good manners. This can have a major impact on our lives, but more importantly, this is the right way for us to treat the Lord and one another. This will also help us prepare for eternity, where we can be sure everyone's manners and respect is impeccable.

Chapter Ten
Group Discussion Questions

1. Describe one key area where the Lord has clearly revealed His perfect will for your life. What are you doing right now to align your life with His divine plan for you?

2. Rick highlights the importance of "good manners" at a time when our culture has grown shallow and selfish. How can our treatment of others help to open doors and advance the kingdom of God in their lives?

3. Ask the Holy Spirit to highlight one person in your sphere of influence who has been dishonored or rejected in the past. Intercede for them and look for a way to demonstrate God's love and high regard for them.

Discerning our Role in His Kingdom 11

The Kingdom is at Hand is about recognizing the present moves of God as well as how we can position ourselves to fulfill our roles in them. The Spirit is presently moving in the world and preparing the way for the Lord in so many ways, it is not possible to be a part of all of them. We must discern what our part will be, so we can fit in the right move of God and in the right place. Though we cannot be part of everything the Lord is doing, we can appreciate and receive from all.

Though a broad segment of Christianity may be backsliding and succumbing to the growing darkness of this age, many are still growing in their faith and in the knowledge of the Lord. They will soon become the most powerful witnesses to His light the world has ever seen. If you are reading this, you must be one of them. For you, I pray a deep and increasing love for God and desire to know Him better. This is the most valuable gift we can have at this time.

This will happen for those who esteem their purpose in the Lord as their highest priority in life and demonstrate it by seeking His kingdom above everything else. As the Lord explained when He exhorted us to seek first His kingdom, this is key to Him providing our every need.

In Romans 12:2 we are commanded, **"Do not be conformed to this world, but be transformed by the renewing of your mind, so that you may prove what the will of God is, that which is good and acceptable and perfect."** Virtually every teacher and theologian who has commented on this verse has seen three levels of the will of God. Doing what is good and acceptable may be the will of God, but we should seek the perfect will of God.

These also correspond to the thirty, sixty, and hundredfold fruit we can produce (see Mark 4:20). God's good and acceptable will is good and acceptable, but His perfect will produce the most fruit. As we have discussed, the Lord will bless anything He can that is done in His name, but there's a big difference between what He will bless and what He will inhabit. Our "high calling" (see Philippians 3:14) is higher than just doing what the Lord will bless; we want to be His dwelling place.

We can see these three levels of God's dwelling places in Scripture—in the tabernacle of Moses and temples which were built to comply with His dimensions, and in

His church. There was an outer court, which any of God's people could enter, so long as they came through the door which represented Jesus. The light in the outer court was natural, and the acacia wood that represented humanity was exposed. Such is the majority of Christianity.

As we see in Revelation 11:2, at the end of this age, this part of God's dwelling place will be removed. There will come a time when those who are content with God's good and acceptable will can no longer hold on to Him. However, this is not something we should fear, so long as we remain devoted to growing in Him.

The second compartment of the tabernacle was the Holy Place. Only the priests could enter this place to perform the divine "service" (see Hebrews 9:6). Virtually all ministry in the outer court was for the people, but the ministry in the Holy Place was to the Lord. Much of the ministry to the Lord was for or on behalf of the people, but it was to the Lord, so most people did not see or know what was happening. As we mature in the Lord and begin to see and walk in our priestly calling, this will become a natural transition in our lives.

The walls of the Holy Place were also made with acacia wood, which represented humanity. However, they were overlaid with pure gold and covered with drapes embroidered with angelic majesties representing the heavenly realm. There was no natural light in the Holy Place, only the light of the lampstand that burned olive oil, representing the Holy Spirit. Few Christians have experienced this reality, but we all can and will if we continue to grow and mature in the Lord.

Though few Christians have served in the Holy Place, some have briefly peeked into the spiritual realm and have often retreated in terror. It is a strange and wonderful place. We are called to be more at home in this realm than in the natural realm. The revelation of the heavenly majesties can be scary, but a good scare that can help us embrace the humility to which God gives grace. Those who have embraced and walked in their priestly duties must learn to enter this place "continually" performing the divine service (see Hebrews 13:15).

As we see in Revelation 11:2, when the outer court is removed, all Christians will perform their priestly duties either on this level or on the next—in the spiritual Holy of Holies where the presence of the Lord is. The spiritual realm may seem strange to us now, but as we continue to mature and grow, we'll realize this is what we were made for, and we'll feel more at home there than in any other place.

Since we have become "new creations" (see II Corinthians 5:17), we should feel more at home in the Spirit than we ever did in the natural realm. From here, the great demonstrations of the powers of the age to come can come, as the kingdom of this world become the kingdoms of our Lord (see Revelation 11:15).

Of the three dwelling places of God, the innermost room was the Holy of Holies, where the ark of the covenant stood and where the manifest presence of the Lord dwelled. Only the high priest could go in this room once a year with the blood of the sacrifice. Our High Priest is Jesus. He is the One who made the sacrifice and took His blood before the Father. We can only enter this room as we abide in Him, which we are all called to do.

The Holy of Holies represents the highest place and highest calling in Christ. Here we are told the mercy seat was overlaid with pure gold "inside and outside" (see Exodus 37:2, 6). Gold represents God's divine nature. By going through the tabernacle, we see the closer we get to the manifest presence of the Lord, the more gold and divine nature we must have, until our nature also becomes pure "inside and outside."

By seeing the glory of the Lord with an unveiled face, we are changed to become like Him (see II Corinthians

3:18). Therefore, our ultimate devotion must be to see Him, while having any veils that might distort His glory removed.

In Revelation 11:2, we see there will come a time when the outer court will no longer be measured as part of the Lord's temple but will be given to the nations to be "tread under foot." This is the only part of the temple the world sees. This also represents institutional Christianity, which will be taken over by the nations. However, at that time, those who are true to the Lord and serve Him will be in the Holy Place and Holy of Holies, which the world in general will not know. This is for an appointed time, and we need not be too concerned with this now.

Much of the work of the harvest will be in this outer court. Just as all the priests served in outer court ministry, even if they also served in the Holy Place, we should all have some ministry on this level, no matter how much we have matured in Christ. Most of what is considered "ministry" today is in fact outer court ministry, which should not be demeaned as less valuable. All ministry for and to the Lord and to His people is valuable and should be highly esteemed.

What we should do now—and should have been doing all along—is continuing to serve at every level while maturing, so we no longer neglect the Holy Place ministry as many have. In Hebrews 9:6, we are told, **"when these things have been so prepared, the priests are continually entering the outer tabernacle performing the divine worship."** The "outer tabernacle" here is not the outer court but the first room of the tabernacle itself, which is the Holy Place.

The mature minister will come boldly before the throne of God, not on their own merit, but carrying the blood of Jesus, whose blood alone gives them access. We should also give ourselves continually to ministry in the Holy Place in the presence of angelic majesties, remembering our service is to the Lord. As we learn to do this, our ministry in the outer court, in the harvest where people are led to the Lord, to the cross represented by the altar, and to the cleansing represented by the laver, we will become far more powerful and effective because we have been with the Lord.

Before the outer court is removed, it will be used as a focal point of a harvest and ingathering of souls like the world has never seen. A mature Christian will minister in all three levels. However, ministry to the Lord must remain the foundation upon which all other ministry is based.

Since our ministry to the Lord is so wonderful and fulfilling, it's easy to become so focused on it that we neglect our ministry to people, which we also must do. Without our continued ministry in the outer court, we will become unbalanced and prideful in a most dangerous way.

When Jesus walked the earth, He continued His ministry to the multitudes while giving special attention to His disciples who would function on a much higher level with Him. Beware of the pride of thinking we are now serving on a level too high to be out among the people and serve even the least of these (see Matthew 25:40). This is also serving Him. If we only serve those who are going higher and not the multitudes, we will become unbalanced. If we only serve the multitudes who are coming to Him and not those who are going higher, we will become unbalanced. We must do both.

We must also learn to enjoy ministry on every level. There is a special joy in seeing new believers become enlightened and learn about the Lord. We should never lose this joy, though it may not compare with ministering in the spiritual realm with angels and other majesties, and nothing can compare with ministering to the Lord Himself. We must cherish each in its time.

Chapter Eleven
Group Discussion Questions

1. We are changed by beholding the glory of the Lord's face. What aspects of God's divine character and nature are you most drawn to? What does this say about your own calling?

2. Rick warns against spiritual elitism in this chapter. What is the best way to cultivate the kind of humility, love, and service towards others for which this chapter calls?

3. We have access to the Most Holy Place through the blood of Christ, not through our own efforts. How do you apply the blood of Christ or remember His atoning sacrifice in your daily prayer life?

THE WEIGHTIEST MATTER 12

On June 6, 2007, I saw the heavens open and a ball of fire, like a meteorite, coming straight for me. As I moved to dodge it, it reacted instantly, so I knew I could not escape. It hit me in the chest, and though I did not feel anything physically, fire went all over and within me. It burned but not physically. It was a spiritual fire that I felt in my heart, not my body. I also felt exhilarated by it, refreshed, and quickened.

Then, I saw the most beautiful bridal gown I had ever seen suspended above me. It was made of other-worldly material. It was the purest white, but it also emitted the most beautiful blue and gold. I could not imagine that a more beautiful gown had ever been made. I heard the voice of the Lord say, "Will you help My bride put this on?" Then the vision ended.

The next day I saw the heavens open again, and I saw the ball of fire again. As I looked, understanding was given to me. The ball of fire was traveling through deep space. There was such a freshness and newness to everything, I knew I was seeing this ball of fire at the beginning of creation. There was also great joy and beauty like that of a beautiful spring morning, even in space. Everything seemed to just emanate beauty, joy, and freshness.

As I kept looking at this ball of fire, I saw into it. At its core was another ball that was a blue/gold metal. This was the nuclear center that caused the fire, which was like a nuclear reaction coming from this inner sphere. This ball was made of the most dense, heavy matter possible. It was also the weightiest thing that mattered to God—His desire for His bride.

I knew this was why I was struck by the ball of fire before being shown the bridal gown. The main fire, the main passion of God, is for His bride.

I was being shown this at the beginning of creation because I needed to understand this was the main thing on God's heart when He created the universe—His bride, who would be His eternal companion. I knew I was given this vision to understand the ages and ages in which this fire had existed without change, but also to understand both His patience and resolve to have His bride. This is the main reason He created the universe, and the main reason for its existence.

God loves His creation, both the spiritual and the natural. He loves every angel and creature, which is why

He notices when even a single sparrow falls to the ground. Still, His first love is for His bride. Though He loves the earth and all creation, His bride was on His heart when He became a man and when He went to the cross.

As I continued to watch the ball of fire, I understood why it burned me spiritually but not physically. This fire does not consume matter because its source is spiritual; it is a heart fire. It is what burns on God's heart, gives life, and is the source of all life. This is why eternal life is to know Him, which is to know His heart. This was the fire which was in the burning bush through which God spoke to Moses. The passion that burns on God's heart for His people is what was imparted to Moses. There is so much life in this fire, which has burned from eternity. It imparted such life to Moses, when God took him at 120 years old, he had not physically deteriorated.

This is also the fire that accompanies the true baptism in the Holy Spirit. It is the passion for what is on God's heart. It is now coming to the earth again because it's time for God's people to be set free, to leave their bondages and cross over to their promised land, their inheritance. It was this fire which also touched Abraham and Sarah, giving them the vision to leave all they knew in Ur to pursue God's purpose.

This fire was the smoking oven that Abraham saw when God sealed His covenant with him. This fire in their hearts gave such life to them that even when Sarah was ninety years old, she was still so physically beautiful that Abraham feared he would be killed by a king who would want her for himself. When we get close enough to God to be touched by what burns on His heart, life is imparted and renewed, not destroyed. This is also why the apostle John lived so long; he laid his head on God's breast and heard His heartbeat. Because John's heart was so close to God's heart, the indestructible life of God permeated him.

Moses was not rejuvenated just by seeing or being close to the burning bush, but by taking upon his own heart what was on God's heart. Again, this is a heart fire, a spiritual fire. We are rejuvenated, not by seeing or being physically close to the fire, but by uniting with what is on His heart. What is burning on the heart of God has been there from eternity; it is indestructible and will never die. As we take what is on His heart to ours, that same indestructible life is in us. This is what it really means to know God, to know the deepest things on His heart, and to share these with Him in His ultimate purposes. We do not need to have a prophetic experience to do this; we just need to be a seeker of God. The true seekers of God, those who are truly close to Him, will burn with a fire that is unquenchable. They will not be lukewarm.

Again, there is nothing weightier, there is nothing that has more substance, energy, power, or life in it than being united with God in what is on His heart. This is the ultimate quest of man, to be one with God, to have His heart. It says in Psalm 103:7, **"He made known His ways to Moses, His acts to the sons of Israel."** Moses was used to performing some of the greatest miracles God has performed through a man, yet Moses wanted to know God's ways, not just His acts. He wanted to be united with the Lord in what was on His heart, not just knowing what He was doing. We also see this in Exodus 33:12-16:

"Then Moses said to the Lord, "See, You say to me, 'Bring up this people' But You have not let me know whom You will send with me. Yet You have said, 'I know you by name, and you have also found grace in My sight.'

"Now therefore, I pray, have, if I have found grace in Your sight, show me now Your way, that I may know You and that I may find grace in Your sight. And consider that this nation is Your people."

And He said, "My presence shall go with you, and I will give you rest."

Then he said to Him, "If Your presence does not go with us, do not lead us up from here.

"For how then will it be known that Your people and I have found grace in Your sight, except You go

with us? So we shall be separate, Your people and I, from all the people who are upon the face of the earth" (NKJV).

This is one of the most basic truths that must be recovered by the church, so she can come into her full purpose and stature and become the pure and spotless bride He is worthy to have. Programs and good works may be noble endeavors because we were also created for good works, but they are not the main thing. The main thing is to love God and to love what He loves, and hate what He hates.

The basic calling for every Christian is to become like Him and do the works He did. We become like Him by seeing His glory, **"But we all, with unveiled face beholding as in a mirror the glory of the Lord, are being transformed into the same image from glory to glory, just as from the Lord, the Spirit" (II Corinthians 3:18).** The works come from His nature. He not only wants to use us to heal the sick, but also to heal the sick for the same reason He did; He loves people. However, if we do not love God more than we love people, we will not love people the way we should.

It has been said that anyone will quit except for the one who is in love. Commitment, duty, honor, devotion to good works, and devotion to the truth are all good things that can help keep us on the path of life, but when the ultimate test comes, only those who love will stand and only those who love will stay the course.

The greatest passion of God, the fire that burns in His heart, is for His bride, the church. This fire will touch the earth again, and those who are His messengers will burn with it. They will arise with this passion to see the bride make herself ready. A new breed of ministry is being commissioned now. These are the true friends of the bridegroom. These will be spiritual eunuchs for the sake of the kingdom. Eunuchs cannot have a desire for the bride or use her for their own purposes; rather, their whole satisfaction comes from seeing the King's satisfaction with His bride; this will be their passion.

This new breed of ministry will not rape the bride; their whole purpose will be to help the bride make herself ready for the King. This new breed of ministry will not use people to build their ministries, they will use their ministries to build people. This will result in a revolution in the church. Selfish ambition will be driven from the ministry of the church. Christians will begin to love each other and serve from love. The result of this will be a society of saints who will become a marvel in the earth and a true light to the world.

Those who understand the times are not nearly as focused on what the devil is doing as they are on what the Lord is doing. The greatest sign the end of the age is near will be the bride emerging in the glory in which she is called to walk. The Lord will not come until His bride is ready. Her preparation for the greatest of all events, the union of Christ with His bride, will accelerate as we draw closer to the end of this age.

As I shared above, the bridal gown was beyond anything of beauty I had ever seen on any garment. Not only was it made of an other-worldly material, it was also fashioned by artists of other-worldly gifts. This, too, is an important message. These gifts are being given to the church to help the bride get ready.

In the Old Testament we often find quotes saying that the Spirit of God came on someone, such as we see in II Chronicles 15:1 or II Chronicles 24:20. However, it was Bezalel who was the first person in the Bible of whom it was said he was **"filled with the Spirit,"** which we see in Exodus 31:2-5, where the Lord told Moses:

"See, I have called by name Bezalel, the son of Uri, the son of Hur, of the tribe of Judah.
I have filled him with the Spirit of God in wisdom, in understanding, in knowledge, and in all kinds of craftsmanship,

to make artistic designs for work in gold, in silver, and in bronze,

and in the cutting of stones for settings, and in the carving of wood, that he may work in all kinds of craftsmanship."

Think about this fact: An artist was the first person to be filled with the Holy Spirit, not a priest, king, or prophet. This should give us a definite sense of the importance the Lord gave to art. His dwelling place, the tabernacle, which is a blueprint or model for the church, the "dwelling place not made with hands," had to be fashioned by the best of all artists. There is a power in art the church has not generally recognized for centuries now. It must be recovered because the Lord is giving artists in His house unprecedented power to prophesy through their art.

When we look at nature, a sunset, or a snowflake, it is obvious there is no artist like God. It is His nature. However, all the beauty we see was made from His love for mankind. It is a gift. This love motivated His art. If you have ever seen a sunset or something of great beauty and had a sense it was made especially for you to see—it was. God's art is for His people. The reverse is about to become true; the highest art of mankind will come from a love for God.

There is an anointing coming upon artists that is even greater than what was given to Bezalel for building the tabernacle of Moses. That was but a type; what is coming is the fulfillment. The glory of the new covenant is greater than the former, and what is given to help adorn the bride will be greater than what came to help adorn the type. We will not continue to look back at the great masters in history; the greatest masters of all will be today.

An anointing is about to come on artists that will be from the Holy Spirit. Art will again be motivated by a love for God. This art will have a prophetic power such as has not been given to mankind before. The more pure the love, the more pure and powerful the art will be. These are gifts from God to His bride, and they will touch her in profound ways to draw her heart to Him and be used to express her heart for Him.

The truest art will always come out of the highest worship, and will be high worship. This is why, at the end of this age, the most creative gifts the world has ever seen will come from the church. These will be part of the garment she will wear, and what she wears will reflect what is in her heart. She will see His glory, she will reflect His glory, and she will produce glory in all she does. Glory will be her garment, and it will be like a train that follows after her.

The Hebrew word for glory is *kabowd* which literally means "weight." The ultimate glory of the bride is the weightiest thing in all creation; it is the love the Lord has for her. Her true glory is she was in the Lord's heart from the beginning; it has never changed and never will. She is the passion of God. Because of this there will be a whole new revelation of the coming wedding feast. The greatest joy of creation will be to see the Creator's joy in His bride. This is the joy that will begin to motivate this new breed of ministry, some of whom will also be the greatest artisans of all time, and will be truly filled with the Spirit.

I am not just talking about painters, sculptors, or musicians in this art, but the true apostles, prophets, evangelists, pastors, and teachers, who were given for the equipping of the saints to become the church we are called to be. They will be so creative in their ministries that ministry will become one of the most compelling attractions of all. This crafting of words in messages will come with such creative power that multitudes will be drawn to their oratory. This is not about entertainment but an anointing on the art of speaking through which the Word of God is worthy to be adorned.

Creativity, the basic nature of the blessed Creator, will shine through His church as a witness of His nature. Because her heart will be in such unity with the Creator, creativity will flow from everything she does. The greatest music, the greatest art of every kind, will come from the church as worship to the Lord. These gifts will also both draw and equip the bride for her highest purpose—her union with the King. It will begin to draw the nations to the feast.

This prophetic experience has reoriented my understanding of some basic issues. From the beginning of my Christian life, I have had an understanding of the importance of the church and how essential a healthy local church life is to true Christian maturity and to being positioned to fulfill our purpose on earth. Therefore, I have always sought to build the local church in all I do, and to keep a heart for the whole body of Christ. Still, before, I had seen the church as a means to an end; the means for preparing the way for the kingdom to come. This is her calling, of course, but not her main purpose. I saw the kingdom as a higher purpose, but that has been reversed—the church is now the higher purpose.

This may seem subtle, and I do not think it will change my teachings, so much as it will change my devotion and orientation. I now have a fire on me for the church I have never had before. I feel a burning desire to see her become all she is called to be, and to be the bride our King is worthy to have.

I think it is more important to have an understanding of the kingdom; it is crucial. The kingdom was the message the Lord came to preach, and the gospel of the kingdom must be preached before the end of this age can come. However, the way we can best help prepare for the kingdom is to help the church become what she is called to be.

The Lord will not come back to set up His kingdom until His bride is ready for Him and ready to rule and reign with Him in His kingdom. The Lord loves the earth and all it contains. He will restore it to its original purpose as a true paradise, but the bride makes His heart beat faster, and the main reason for creation is for Him to enjoy it with His bride.

We may think if the church sees this, it will become arrogant and egocentric, but there are enough forces in the world determined to keep her humble. She needs to see her high purpose to start living in a manner worthy of her calling. Christians, as the church, are the true royalty in the earth, and she must start to carry herself with the dignity and respect of her most royal blood. Of course, this is not to be served, but to serve, and to do it with all the authority she has been given.

Consequently, one of the most important things any of us can do is find our place in His church, and begin to do all we can to help her become ready for Him. The true friends of the Bridegroom will never give up on this because they love Him. They will not let any disappointments or discouragements deter them from this purpose. The Lord will have a worthy bride, and those who love will never quit until He does. This is the new breed.

A few days after I received this revelation, I shared it with Bob Jones. He immediately related it to an astronomical discovery of which I was not aware—the recent discovery of "the father of all supernovas." The heavens were given for signs (see Genesis 1:14; Psalm 19). This is a major sign and a timely one. It is believed that at the heart of a supernova there is matter so dense, so heavy, that a teardrop amount of it would have more weight than all human beings on earth. This matter is so heavy and has such gravitational pull that it creates "black holes." This supergravity even keeps light from escaping it. This supernova is supposed to be much larger than any previously discovered. If it is the greatest of all, then the weightiest matter in creation would be at the center of it. That is what I saw in the middle of the ball of fire—the weightiest matter in the universe because it is what matters most to God.

This discovery is no accident, and its timing is prophetic. I expect those who gaze into the true heavens will likewise discover this weightiest of all matters, the Lord's love for His bride. Just as supernovas create the biggest explosions in the universe and the greatest light emitted in the universe before they become the "black hole" by the denseness of their gravity, I expect a similar explosion of greater power than has been released before, and greater light than has ever been seen before through the church. By this, she will be transformed quickly into all she is called to be.

The earth hardly even qualifies as a speck of dust in the expanse of the universe. Why would it be given such importance? As King David pondered in Psalm 8, what is man that God would even consider any of us? He is looking for a bride, a companion, with which to share His creation; to share eternity. That is your calling. There is no higher calling in all creation than to be a part of His bride, the church. She will even ultimately judge angels, sharing His authority, sitting on His throne with Him. As we get closer to Him, we will begin to walk in this.

Again, the main thing we can do to help the earth in a permanent and lasting way is to help the church become what she is called to be. The most effective way we can do this is by loving God more, knowing Him better, abiding in Him, and directing the church's attention to who He is. The church is in desperate need of knowing who she is called to be. However, it is not by knowing who we are in Christ that we will be changed, but by knowing who He is in us. We do not want to worship the temple of the Lord but the Lord of the temple. Still, as we come to understand His love for His bride, we will do everything we can to help her get ready for Him because we love Him.

Chapter Twelve
Group Discussion Questions

1. The meteor that Rick saw in this encounter "hit him in the chest" which signifies the revelation impacted his heart. What personal revelations or insights about the Lord have impacted your heart the most?

2. How can prophetic encounters enrich or accelerate our pursuit of the kingdom of God? What can you do to incorporate more prophetic activation into your daily routine?

3. Rick remarks that "there is no artist like God" and highlights a sign in the heavens that confirmed his prophetic encounter. What can you do to incorporate God's creation more into your daily pursuit of Him?

Scan the QR below to Join **Rick Joyner's Word for the Week!**

Sign up to receive the MorningStar Journal, Word for the Week and other MorningStar Resources!

Subscribe

The NEW MorningStar Ministries App is here. <u>Download</u> it FREE now!

Give God your gap year and reap the benefits for life.

Join us this coming school year and find your place in the next move of God! Receive in-depth teaching, training, and mentoring in supernatural ministry. We offer one-year ministry certificate programs as well as associate and bachelor degrees with five different majors from which to choose. Our high-impact programs include the Company of Prophets, the School of Worship, Special Forces Missions, the School of Communications, and the School of Revival.

Learn more at: mstaru.com

Made in the USA
Las Vegas, NV
16 December 2023